THE AUTHOR: Yukio Mishima, one of the most spectacularly gifted writers in modern Japan, was born into a samurai family in 1925. He attended the Peers' School and Tokyo Imperial University, and for a time worked at the Ministry of Finance. His first full-length novel, *Confessions of a Mask*, appeared in 1949, and since then he published over a dozen novels, almost all of which were translated into English and other languages during his lifetime. They include: *Thirst for Love*; *Forbidden Colors*; *Death in Midsummer*; *The Sound of Waves*; *The Temple of the Golden Pavilion*; *After the Banquet*; *The Sailor Who Fell from Grace with the Sea*; and *Spring Snow*.

Mishima's reverence for the Japanese martial arts led him to take up Kendo (a type of fencing, with wooden swords) and Karate, as well as body-building, and by 1968 he had become a Kendo master of the fifth *dan*. He also organized a "private army" called the Shield Society, and in November 1970 he and his group forced their way into a Self-Defense Force headquarters in Tokyo, where Mishima, after reading out a proclamation, committed ritual suicide with a young follower in the commanding officer's room. On the morning of his death, the last volume of Mishima's tetralogy, *The Sea of Fertility*, was delivered to his publisher.

He is survived by his wife and two children.

THE TRANSLATOR: John Bester, born and educated in England, is one of the foremost translators of Japanese fiction. Among his translations are Masuji Ibuse's *Black Rain*, Kenzaburo Oe's *The Silent Cry*, Fumiko Enchi's *The Waiting Years*, Junnosuke Yoshiyuki's *The Dark Room*, and seven stories by Mishima entitled *Acts of Worship* (for which he received the 1990 Noma Award for the Translation of Japanese Literature).

Sun & Steel

YUKIO MISHIMA

Translated by JOHN BESTER

KODANSHA INTERNATIONAL

Tokyo and New York

Distributed in the United States by Kodansha International/ USA Ltd., 114 Fifth Avenue, New York, NY 10011. Published by Kodansha International Ltd., 17-14, Otowa 1-chome, Bunkyo-ku, Tokyo 112 and Kodansha International/USA Ltd. Copyright © 1970 by Kodansha International Ltd. All rights reserved. Printed in Japan.
LCC 76-100628
ISBN 0-87011-425-5 (U.S.)
ISBN 4-7700-0796-5 (Japan)
First edition, 1970
First paperback edition, 1980
Fourth printing, 1990

Of late, I have come to sense within myself an accumulation of all kinds of things that cannot find adequate expression via an objective artistic form such as the novel. A lyric poet of twenty might manage it, but I am twenty no longer, and have never been a poet at any rate. I have groped around, therefore, for some other form more suited to such personal utterances and have come up with a kind of hybrid between confession and criticism, a subtly equivocal mode that one might call "confidential criticism."

I see it as a twilight genre between the night of confession and the daylight of criticism. The "I" with which I shall occupy myself will not be the "I" that relates back strictly to myself, but something else, some residue, that remains after all the other words I have uttered have flowed back into me, something that neither relates back nor flows back.

As I pondered the nature of that "I," I was driven to the conclusion that the "I" in question corresponded precisely with the physical space that I occupied. What I was seeking, in short, was a language of the body.

If my self was my dwelling, then my body resembled an orchard that surrounded it. I could either cultivate that orchard to its capacity or leave it for the weeds to run riot in. I was free to choose, but the freedom was not as obvious as it might seem. Many people, indeed, go so far as to refer to the orchards of their dwellings as "destiny."

One day, it occurred to me to set about cultivating my

orchard for all I was worth. For my purpose, I used sun and steel. Unceasing sunlight and implements fashioned of steel became the chief elements in my husbandry. Little by little, the orchard began to bear fruit, and thoughts of the body came to occupy a large part of my consciousness.

All this did not occur, of course, overnight. Nor did it begin without the existence of some deep-lying motive.

When I examine closely my early childhood, I realise that my memory of words reaches back far farther than my memory of the flesh. In the average person, I imagine, the body precedes language. In my case, words came first of all; then—belatedly, with every appearance of extreme reluctance, and already clothed in concepts—came the flesh. It was already, as goes without saying, sadly wasted by words.

First comes the pillar of plain wood, then the white ants that feed on it. But for me, the white ants were there from the start, and the pillar of plain wood emerged tardily, already half eaten away.

Let the reader not chide me for comparing my own trade to the white ant. In its essence, any art that relies on words makes use of their ability to eat away—of their corrosive function—just as etching depends on the corrosive power of nitric acid. Yet the simile is not accurate enough; for the copper and the nitric acid used in etching are on a par with each other, both being extracted from nature, while the relation of words to reality is not that of the acid to the plate. Words are a medium that reduces reality to abstraction for transmission to our reason, and in their power to corrode reality inevitably lurks the danger that the words themselves will be corroded too. It might be more appropriate, in fact, to liken their action to that of excess stomach fluids that digest and gradually eat away the stomach itself.

Many people will express disbelief that such a process could already be at work in a person's earliest years. But that, beyond doubt, is what happened to me personally, thereby laying the ground for two contradictory tendencies within myself. One was the determination to press ahead loyally with the corrosive function of words, and to make that my life's work. The other was the desire to encounter reality in some field where words should play no part at all.

In a more "healthy" process of development, the two tendencies can often work together without conflict, even in the case of a born writer, giving rise to a highly desirable state of affairs in which a training in words leads to a fresh discovery of reality. But the emphasis here is on rediscovery; if this is to happen, it is necessary, at the outset of life, to have possessed the reality of the flesh still unsullied by words. And that is quite different from what happened to me.

My composition teacher would often show his displeasure with my work, which was innocent of any words that might be taken as corresponding to reality. It seems that, in my childish way, I had an unconscious presentiment of the subtle, fastidious laws of words, and was aware of the necessity of avoiding as far as possible coming into contact with reality via words if one was to profit from their positive corrosive function and escape their negative aspect—if, to put it more simply, one was to maintain the purity of words. I knew instinctively that the only possibility was to maintain a constant watch on the corrosive action lest it suddenly come up against some object that it might corrode.

The natural corollary of such a tendency was that I should openly admit the existence of reality and the body only in fields where words had no part whatsoever; thus reality and the body became synonymous for me, the objects, almost, of a kind of fetishism. Without doubt, too, I was quite unconsciously expanding my interest in words to embrace this interest also; and this type of fetishism corresponded exactly to my fetish for words.

In the first stage, I was quite obviously identifying myself with words and setting reality, the flesh, and action on the other side. There is no doubt, either, that my prejudice concerning words was encouraged by this wilfully created antinomy, and that my deep-rooted misunderstanding of the nature of reality, the flesh, and action was formed in the same way.

This antinomy rested on the assumption that I myself from the outset was devoid of the flesh, of reality, of action. It was true, indeed, that the flesh came late to me at the beginning, but I was waiting for it with words.

I suspect that because of the earlier tendency I spoke of, I did not perceive it, then, as "my body." If I had done so, my words would have lost their purity. I should have been violated by reality, and reality would have become inescapable.

Interestingly enough, my stubborn refusal to perceive the body was itself due to a beautiful misconception in my idea of what the body was. I did not know that a man's body never shows itself as "existence." But as I saw things, it ought to have made itself apparent, clearly and unequivocally, as existence. It naturally followed that when it did show itself unmistakably as a terrifying paradox of existence—as a form of existence that rejected existence—I was as panic-stricken as though I had come across some monster, and loathed it accordingly. It never occurred to me that other men—all men without exception—were the same.

It is perhaps only natural that this type of panic and fear, though so obviously the product of a misconception, should postulate another more desirable physical existence, another more desirable reality. Never dreaming that the body existing in a form that rejected existence was universal in the male, I set about constructing my ideal hypothetical physical existence by investing it with all the opposite characteristics. And since my own, abnormal bodily existence was doubtless a product of the intellectual corrosion of words, the ideal body—the ideal existence—must, I told myself, be absolutely free from any interference by words. Its characteristics could be summed up as taciturnity and beauty of form.

At the same time, I decided that if the corrosive power of words had any creative function, it must find its model in the formal beauty of this "ideal body," and that the ideal in the verbal arts must lie solely in the imitation of such physical beauty—in other words, the pursuit of a beauty that was absolutely free from corrosion.

This was an obvious self-contradiction, since it represented an attempt to deprive words of their essential function and to strip reality of its essential characteristics. Yet, in another sense, it was an exceedingly clever and artful method of ensuring that words and the reality they should have dealt with never came face to face.

In this way my mind, without realizing what it was doing, straddled these two contradictory elements and, godlike, set about trying to manipulate them. It was thus that I started writing novels. And this increased still further my thirst for reality and the flesh.

Later, much later, thanks to the sun and the steel, I was to learn the language of the flesh, much as one might learn a foreign language. It was my second language, an aspect of my spiritual development. My purpose now is to talk of that development. As a personal history, it will, I suspect, be unlike anything seen before, and as such exceedingly difficult to follow.

When I was small, I would watch the young men parade the portable shrine through the streets at the local shrine festival. They were intoxicated with their task, and their expressions were of an indescribable abandon, their faces averted; some of them even rested the backs of their necks against the shafts of the shrine they shouldered, so that their eyes gazed up at the heavens. And my mind was much troubled by the riddle of what it was that those eyes reflected.

As to the nature of the intoxicating vision that I detected in all this violent physical stress, my imagination provided no clue. For many a month, therefore, the enigma continued to occupy my mind; it was only much later, after I had begun to learn the language of the flesh, that I undertook to help in shouldering a portable shrine, and was at last able to solve the puzzle that had plagued me since infancy. They were simply looking at the sky. In their eyes there was no vision: only the reflection of the blue and absolute skies of early autumn. Those blue skies, though, were unusual skies such as I might never see again in my life: one moment strung up high aloft, the next plunged to the depths; constantly shifting, a strange compound of lucidity and madness.

I promptly set down what I had discovered in a short essay, so important did my experience seem to me.

In short, I had found myself at a point where there were no grounds for doubting that the sky that my own poetic intuition had shown me, and the sky revealed to the eyes of those ordinary young men of the neighborhood, were identical. That moment for which I had been waiting so long was a blessing that the sun and the steel had conferred on me. Why, you may ask, were there no grounds for doubt? Because, provided certain physical conditions are equal and a certain physical burden shared, so long as an equal physical stress is savored and an identical intoxication overtakes all alike, then differences of individual sensibility are restricted by countless factors to an absolute minimum. If, in addition, the introspective element is removed almost completely—then one is safe in asserting that what I had witnessed was no individual illusion, but one fragment of a well-defined group vision. My "poetic intuition" did not become a personal privilege until later, when I used words to recall and reconstruct that vision; my eyes, in their meeting with the blue sky, had penetrated to the essential *pathos* of the doer.

And in that swaying blue sky that, like a fierce bird of prey with wings outstretched, alternately swept down and soared upwards to infinity, I perceived the true nature of what I had long referred to as "tragic."

According to my definition of tragedy, the tragic *pathos* is born when the perfectly average sensibility momentarily takes unto itself a privileged nobility that keeps others at a distance, and not when a special type of sensibility vaunts its own special claims. It follows that he who dabbles in words can create tragedy, but cannot participate in it. It is necessary, moreover, that the "privileged nobility" find its basis strictly in a kind of physical courage. The elements of intoxication and superhuman clarity in the tragic are born when the average sensibility, endowed with a given physical strength, encounters that type of privileged moment especially designed for it. Tragedy calls for an anti-tragic vitality and ignorance, and above all for a certain "inappropriateness." If a person is at times to draw close to the divine, then under normal conditions he must be neither divine nor anything approaching it.

It was only when I, in my turn, saw the strange, divine blue sky perceived only by that type of person, that I at last trusted the universality of my own sensibility, that my thirst was slaked, and that my morbidly blind faith in words was dispelled. At that moment, I participated in the tragedy of all being.

Once I had gazed upon this sight, I understood all kinds of things hitherto unclear to me. The exercise of the muscles elucidated the mysteries that words had made. It was similar to the process of acquiring erotic knowledge. Little by little, I began to understand the feeling behind existence and action.

If that were all, it would merely mean that I had trodden somewhat belatedly the same path as other people. I had another scheme of my own, however. Insofar as the spirit was concerned—I told myself—there was nothing especially out of the way in the idea of some particular thought invading my spirit, enlarging it, and eventually occupying the whole of it. Since, however, I was gradually beginning to weary of the dualism of flesh and spirit, it naturally occurred to me to wonder why such an incident should occur within the spirit and come to an end at its outer fringes. There are, of course, many cases of psychosomatic diseases where the spirit extends its domain to the body. But what I was considering went further than this. Granted that my flesh in infancy had made itself apparent in intellectual guise, corroded by words, then should it not be possible to reverse the process—to extend the scope of an idea from the spirit to the flesh until the whole physical being became a suit of armor forged from the metal of that concept?

The idea in question, as I have already suggested in my definition of tragedy, resolved itself into the concept of the body. And it seemed to me that the flesh could be "intellectualized" to a higher degree, could achieve a closer intimacy with ideas, than the spirit.

For ideas are, in the long run, essentially foreign to human existence; and the body—receptacle of the involuntary muscles, of the internal organs and circulatory system over which it has no control—is foreign to the spirit, so that it is even possible for people to use the body as a metaphor for ideas, both being something quite alien to human existence as such. And the way in which an idea can take possession of the mind unbidden, with the suddenness of a stroke of fate, reinforces still further the resemblance of ideas to the body with which each of us, willy-nilly, is endowed, giving even this automatic, uncontrollable function a striking resemblance to the flesh. It is this that forms the basis of the idea of the enfleshment of Christ and also the stigmata some people can produce on their palms and insteps.

Nevertheless, the flesh has its limitations. Even should some eccentric idea require that a man sprout a pair of formidable horns on his head, they would obviously refuse to grow. The limiting factors, ultimately, are the harmony and balance on which the body insists. All these do is to provide beauty of the most average kind and the physical qualifications necessary for viewing that swaying sky of the shrine-bearers. They also, it seems, fulfill the function of taking revenge on, and correcting, any excessively eccentric idea. And they constantly draw one back to the point at which there is no longer any room to doubt "one's identity with others." In this way, my body, while itself the product of an idea, would doubtless also serve as the best cloak with which to hide the idea. If the body could achieve perfect, non-individual harmony, then it would be possible to shut individuality up for ever in close confinement. I had always felt that such signs of physical individuality as a bulging belly (sign of spiritual sloth) or a flat chest with protruding ribs (sign of an unduly nervous sensibility) were excessively ugly, and I could not contain my surprise when I discovered that there were people who loved such signs. To me, these could only seem acts of shameless indecency, as though the owner were exposing his spiritual pudenda on the outside of his body. They represented one type of narcissism that I could never forgive.

The theme of the estrangement of body and spirit, born of the craving I have described, persisted for a long time as a principal theme in my work. I only came to take gradual leave of it when I at last began to consider whether it was not possible that the body, too, might have its own logic, possibly even its own thought; when I began to feel that the body's special qualities did not lie solely in taciturnity and beauty of form, but that the body too might have its own loquacity. ←—talkative

When I describe in this fashion the shifts in these two trains of thought, the reader will surely say that I merely start by taking what were, if anything, generally accepted premises and get involved in a maze of illogicality. The estrangement of body and spirit in modern society is an almost universal phenomenon, and there is nobody—the reader may feel—who would fail to deplore it; so that to prate emotionally about the body "thinking" or the "loquacity" of the flesh is going too far, and by using such phrases I am merely covering up my own confusion.

In fact, by setting my fetish for reality and physical existence and my fetish for words on the same level, by making them an exact equation, I had already brought into sight the discovery I was to make later. From the moment I set the wordless body, full of physical beauty, in opposition to beautiful words that imitated physical beauty, thereby equating them as two things springing from one and the same conceptual source, I had in effect, without realizing it, already released myself from the spell of words. For it meant that I was recognizing the identical origin of the formal beauty in the wordless body and the formal beauty in words, and was beginning to seek a kind of platonic idea that would make it possible to put the flesh and words on the same footing. At that stage, the attempt to project words onto the body was already only a stone's throw away. The attempt itself, of course, was strikingly unplatonic, but there remained only one more experience for me to pass through before I could start to talk of the ideas of the flesh and the loquacity of the body.

In order to explain what that was, I must start by describing the encounter between myself and the sun.

In fact, this experience occurred on two occasions. It often happens that, long before the decisive meeting with a person from whom only death can thereafter part one, there is a brief brush elsewhere with that same person occurring with almost total unawareness on both sides. So it was with my encounter with the sun.

My first—unconscious—encounter was in the summer of the defeat, in the year 1945. A relentless sun blazed down on the lush grass of that summer that lay on the borderline between the war and the postwar period— a borderline, in fact, that was nothing more than a line of barbed wire entanglements, half broken down, half buried in the summer weeds, tilting in all directions. I walked in the sun's rays, but had no clear understanding of the meaning they held for me.

Finespun and impartial, the summer sunlight poured down prodigally on all creation alike. The war ended, yet the deep green weeds were lit exactly as before by the merciless light of noon, a clearly perceived hallucination stirring in a slight breeze; brushing the tips of the leaves with my fingers, I was astonished that they did not vanish at my touch.

That same sun, as the days turned to months and the months to years, had become associated with a pervasive corruption and destruction. In part, it was the way it gleamed so encouragingly on the wings of planes leaving on missions, on forests of bayonets, on the badges of military caps, on the embroidery of military banners; but still more, far more, it was the way it glistened on the blood flowing ceaselessly from the flesh, and on the silver bodies of flies clustering on wounds. Holding sway over corruption, leading youth in droves to its death in tropical seas and countrysides, the sun lorded it over that vast rusty-red ruin that stretched away to the distant horizon.

I little dreamed—since the sun had never been disassociated from the image of death—that it could ever confer on me a bodily blessing, even though it had, of course, long harbored images of radiant glory. . . .

I was already fifteen, and I had written a poem:

> And still the light
> Pours down; men laud the day.
> I shun the sun and cast my soul
> Into the shadowy pit.

How dearly, indeed, I loved my pit, my dusky room, the area of my desk with its piles of books! How I enjoyed introspection, shrouded myself in cogitation; with what rapture did I listen for the rustling of frail insects in the thickets of my nerves!

A hostility towards the sun was my only rebellion against the spirit of the age. I hankered after Novalis's night and Yeatsian Irish twilights. However, from the time the war ended, I gradually sensed that an era was approaching in which to treat the sun as an enemy would be tantamount to following the herd.

The literary works written or put before the public around that time were dominated by night thoughts— though their night was far less aesthetic than mine. To be really respected at that time, moreover, one's darkness had to be rich and cloying, not thin. Even the rich honeyed night in which I myself had wallowed in my boyhood seemed to them, apparently, very thin stuff indeed.

Little by little, I began to feel uncertain about the night in which I had placed such trust during the war, and to suspect that I might have belonged with the sun worshippers all along. It may well have been so. And if it was indeed so—I began to wonder—might not my persistent hostility towards the sun, and the continued importance I attached to my own small private night, be no more than a desire to follow the herd?

The men who indulged in nocturnal thought, it seemed to me, had without exception dry, lusterless skins and sagging stomachs. They sought to wrap up a whole epoch in a capacious night of ideas, and rejected in all its forms the sun that I had seen. They rejected both life and death as I had seen them, for in both of these the sun had had a hand.

It was in 1952, on the deck of the ship on which I made my first journey abroad, that I exchanged a reconciliatory handshake with the sun. From that day on, I have found myself unable to part company with it. The sun became associated with the main highway of my life. And little by little, it tanned my skin brown, branding me as a member of the other race.

One might object that thought belongs, essentially, to the night, that creation with words is of necessity carried out in the fevered darkness of night. Indeed, I had still not lost my old habit of working through the small hours, and I was surrounded by people whose skins unmistakably bore witness to nocturnal thinking.

Yet why must it be that men always seek out the depths, the abyss? Why must thought, like a plumb line, concern itself exclusively with vertical descent? Why was it not feasible for thought to change direction and climb vertically up, ever up, towards the surface? Why should the area of the skin, which guarantees a human being's existence in space, be most despised and left to the tender mercies of the senses? I could not understand the laws governing the motion of thought—the way it was liable to get stuck in unseen chasms whenever it set out to go deep; or, whenever it aimed at the heights, to soar away into boundless and equally invisible heavens, leaving the corporeal form undeservedly neglected.

If the law of thought is that it should search out profundity, whether it extends upwards or downwards, then it seemed excessively illogical to me that men should not discover depths of a kind in the "surface," that vital borderline that endorses our separateness and our form, dividing our exterior from our interior. Why should they not be attracted by the profundity of the surface itself?

The sun was enticing, almost dragging, my thoughts away from their night of visceral sensations, away to the swelling of muscles encased in sunlit skin. And it was commanding me to construct a new and sturdy dwelling in which my mind, as it rose little by little to the surface, could live in security. That dwelling was a tanned, lustrous skin and powerful, sensitively rippling muscles. I came to feel that it was precisely because such an abode was required that the average intellectual failed to feel at home with thought that concerned itself with forms and surfaces.

The nocturnal outlook, product of diseased inner organs, is given shape almost before its owner is aware which came first, the outlook itself or those first faint morbid symptoms in the inner organs. And yet, in remote recesses invisible to the eye, the body slowly creates and regulates its own thought. With the surface, on the other hand, which is visible to everybody, training of the body must take precedence over training of thought if it is to create and supervise its own ideas.

The need for me to train my body could have been foreseen from that moment when I first felt the attraction of the surface profundities. I was aware that the only thing that could justify such an idea was muscle. Who pays any attention to a physical education theorist grown decrepit? One might accept the pallid scholar's toying with nocturnal thoughts in the privacy of his study, but what could seem more meager, more chilly than his lips were they to speak, whether in praise or in blame, of the body? So well acquainted was I with poverty of that type that one day, quite suddenly, it occurred to me to acquire ample muscles of my own.

I would draw attention here to one fact: that everything, as this shows, proceeded from my "mind." I believe that just as physical training will transform supposedly involuntary muscles into voluntary ones, so a similar transformation can be achieved through training the mind. Both body and mind, through an inevitable tendency that one might almost call a natural law, are inclined to lapse into automatism, but I have found by experience that a large stream may be deflected by digging a small channel.

This is another example of the quality that our spirits and bodies have in common: that tendency shared by the body and the mind to instantly create their own small universe, their own "false order," whenever, at one particular time, they are taken control of by one particular idea. Although what happens in fact represents a kind of standstill, it is experienced as though it were a burst of lively, centripetal activity. This function of the body and mind in creating for a short while their own miniature universes is, in fact, no more than an illusion; yet the fleeting sense of happiness in human life owes much to precisely this type of "false order." It is a kind of protective function of life in face of the chaos around it, and resembles the way a hedgehog rolls itself up into a tight round ball.

The possibility then presented itself of breaking down one type of "false order" and creating another in its place, of turning back on itself this obstinate formative function and resetting it in a direction that better accorded with one's own aims. This idea, I decided, I would immediately put into action. Rather than "idea," though, I might have said the new purpose which the sun provided me with each day.

It was thus that I found myself confronted with those lumps of steel: heavy, forbidding, cold as though the essence of night had in them been still further condensed.

On that day began my close relationship with steel that was to last for ten years to come.

The nature of this steel is odd. I found that as I increased its weight little by little, the effect was like a pair of scales: the bulk of muscles placed, as it were, on the other pan increased proportionately, as though the steel had a duty to maintain a strict balance between the two. Little by little, moreover, the properties of my muscles came increasingly to resemble those of the steel. This slow development, I found, was remarkably similar to the process of education, which remodels the brain intellectually by feeding it with progressively more difficult matter. And since there was always the vision of a classical ideal of the body to serve as a model and an ultimate goal, the process closely resembled the classical ideal of education.

And yet, which of the two was it that really resembled the other? Was I not already using words in my attempt to imitate the classical physical type? For me, beauty is always retreating from one's grasp: the only thing I consider important is what existed once, or ought to have existed. By its subtle, infinitely varied operation, the steel restored the classical balance that the body had begun to lose, reinstating it in its natural form, the form that it should have had all along.

The groups of muscles that have become virtually unnecessary in modern life, though still a vital element of a man's body, are obviously pointless from a practical point of view, and bulging muscles are as unnecessary as a classical education is to the majority of practical men. Muscles have gradually become something akin to classical Greek. To revive the dead language, the discipline of the steel was required; to change the silence of death into the eloquence of life, the aid of steel was essential.

The steel faithfully taught me the correspondence between the spirit and the body: thus feeble emotions, it seemed to me, corresponded to flaccid muscles, sentimentality to a sagging stomach, and overimpressionability to an oversensitive, white skin. Bulging muscles, a taut stomach, and a tough skin, I reasoned, would correspond respectively to an intrepid fighting spirit, the power of dispassionate intellectual judgement, and a robust disposition. I hasten to point out here that I do not believe ordinary people to be like this. Even my own scanty experience is enough to furnish me with innumerable examples of timid minds encased within bulging muscles. Yet, as I have already pointed out, words for me came before the flesh, so that intrepidity, dispassionateness, robustness, and all those emblems of moral character summed up by words, needed to manifest themselves in outward, bodily tokens. For that reason, I told myself, I ought to endow myself with the physical characteristics in question as a kind of educative process.

Beyond the educative process there also lurked another, romantic design. The romantic impulse that had formed an undercurrent in me from boyhood on, and that made sense only as the *destruction* of classical perfection, lay waiting within me. Like a theme in an operatic overture that is later destined to occur throughout the whole work, it laid down a definitive pattern for me before I had achieved anything in practice.

Specifically, I cherished a romantic impulse towards death, yet at the same time I required a strictly classical body as its vehicle; a peculiar sense of destiny made me believe that the reason why my romantic impulse towards death remained unfulfilled in reality was the immensely simple fact that I lacked the necessary physical qualifications. A powerful, tragic frame and sculpturesque muscles were indispensable in a romantically noble death. Any confrontation between weak, flabby flesh and death seemed to me absurdly inappropriate. Longing at eighteen for an early demise, I felt myself unfitted for it. I lacked, in short, the muscles suitable for a dramatic death. And it deeply offended my romantic pride that it should be this unsuitability that had permitted me to survive the war.

For all that, these purely intellectual convolutions were as yet nothing but the entangling of themes within the prelude to a human life that so far had achieved nothing. It remained for me some day to achieve something, to destroy something. That was where the steel came in— it was the steel that gave me a clue as to how to do so.

At the point at which many people feel satisfied with the degree of intellectual cultivation they have already achieved, I was fated to discover that in my case the intellect, far from being a harmless cultural asset, had been granted me solely as a weapon, as a means of survival. Thus the physical disciplines that later became so necessary to my survival were in a sense comparable to the way in which a person for whom the body has been the only means of living launches into a frantic attempt to acquire an intellectual education when his youth is on its deathbed.

The steel taught me many different things. It gave me an utterly new kind of knowledge, a knowledge that neither books nor worldly experience can impart. Muscles, I found, were strength as well as form, and each complex of muscles was subtly responsible for the direction in which its own strength was exerted, much as though they were rays of light given the form of flesh.

Nothing could have accorded better with the definition of a work of art that I had long cherished than this concept of form enfolding strength, coupled with the idea that a work should be organic, radiating rays of light in all directions.

The muscles that I thus created were at one and the same time simple existence and works of art; they even, paradoxically, possessed a certain abstract nature. Their one fatal flaw was that they were too closely involved with the life process, which decreed that they should decline and perish with the decline of life itself.

This oddly abstract nature I will return to later; more important here is the fact that, for me, muscles had one of the most desirable qualities of all: their function was precisely opposite to that of words. This will become clear if one considers the origin of words themselves. At first, in much the same way as stone coinage, words become current among the members of a race as a universal means to the communication of emotions and needs. So long as they remain unsoiled by handling, they are common property, and they can, accordingly, express nothing but commonly shared emotions.

However, as words become particularized, and as men begin—in however small a way—to use them in personal, arbitrary ways, so their transformation into art begins. It was words of this kind that, descending on me like a swarm of winged insects, seized on my individuality and sought to shut me up within it. Nevertheless, despite the enemy's depredations upon my person, I turned their universality—at once a weapon and a weakness—back on them, and to some extent succeeded in using words to universalize my own individuality.

Yet that success lay in being different from others, and was essentially at variance with the origins and early development of words. Nothing, in fact, is so strange as the glorification of the verbal arts. Seeming at first glance to strive after universality, in fact they concern themselves with subtle ways of betraying the fundamental function of words, which is to be universally applicable. The glorification of individual style in literature signifies precisely that. The epic poems of ancient times are, perhaps, an exception, but every literary work with its author's name standing at its head is no more than a beautiful "perversion of words."

Can the blue sky that we all see, the mysterious blue sky that is seen identically by all the bearers of the festival shrine, ever be given verbal expression?

It was here, as I have already said, that my deepest doubts lay; and conversely what I found in muscles, through the intermediacy of steel, was a burgeoning of this type of triumph of the non-specific, the triumph of knowing that one was the same as others. As the relentless pressure of the steel progressively stripped my muscles of their unusualness and individuality (which were a product of degeneration), and as they gradually developed, they should, I reasoned, begin to assume a universal aspect, until finally they reached a point where they conformed to a general pattern in which individual differences ceased to exist. The universality thus attained would suffer no private corrosion, no betrayal. That was its most desirable trait in my eyes.

In addition, those muscles, so apparent to the eye, so palpable to the touch, began to acquire an abstract quality all their own. Muscles, of which non-communication is the very essence, ought never in theory to acquire the abstract quality common to means of communication. And yet. . . .

One summer day, heated by training, I was cooling my muscles in the breeze coming through an open window. The sweat vanished as though by magic, and coolness passed over the surface of the muscles like a touch of menthol. The next instant, I was rid of the sense of the muscles' existence, and—in the same way that words, by their abstract functioning, can grind up the concrete world so that the words themselves seem never to have existed—my muscles at that moment crushed something within my being, so that it was as though the muscles themselves had similarly never existed.

What was it, then, that they had crushed?

It was that sense of existence in which we normally believe in such a halfhearted manner, which they had transformed into a kind of transparent sense of power. It is this that I refer to as their "abstract nature." As my resort to the steel had persistently suggested to me, the relationship of muscles to steel was one of interdependence: very similar, in fact, to the relationship between ourselves and the world. In short, the sense of existence by which strength cannot be strength without some object represents the basic relationship between ourselves and the world; it is precisely to that extent that we depend on the world, and that I depended on steel. Just as muscles slowly increase their resemblance to steel, so we are gradually fashioned by the world; and although neither the steel nor the world can very well possess a sense of their own existence, idle analogy leads us unwittingly into the illusion that both do, in fact, possess such a sense. Otherwise, we feel powerless to check up on our own sense of existence, and Atlas, for example, would gradually come to regard the globe on his shoulders as something akin to himself. Thus our sense of existence seeks after some object, and can only live in a false world of relativity.

It is true enough that when I lifted a certain weight of steel, I was able to believe in my own strength. I sweated and panted, struggling to obtain certain proof of my strength. At such times, the strength was mine, and equally it was the steel's. My sense of existence was feeding on itself.

Away from the steel, however, my muscles seemed to lapse into absolute isolation, their bulging shapes no more than cogs created to mesh with the steel. The cool breeze passed, the sweat evaporated—and with them the existence of the muscles vanished into thin air. And yet, it was then that the muscles played their most essential function, grinding up with their sturdy, invisible teeth that ambiguous, relative sense of existence and substituting for it an unqualified sense of transparent, peerless power that required no object at all. Even the muscles themselves no longer existed. I was enveloped in a sense of power as transparent as light.

It is scarcely to be wondered at that in this pure sense of power that no amount of books or intellectual analysis could ever capture, I should discover a true antithesis of words. And indeed it was this that by gradual stages was to become the focus of my whole thinking.

The formulation of any new way of thought begins with the trial rephrasing in many different ways of a single, as yet ambiguous theme. As the fisherman tries all kinds of rods, and the fencer all kinds of bamboo swords until he finds one whose length and weight suit him, so, in the formulation of a way of thinking, an as yet imprecise idea is given experimental expression in a variety of forms; only when the right measurements and weight are discovered does it become part of oneself.

When I experienced that pure sense of strength, I had a presentiment that here at last was the future focus of my thought. The idea gave me indescribable pleasure, and I looked forward to dallying with it in a leisurely fashion before appropriating it to myself as a way of thinking. I would take my time, spinning out the process, taking care to prevent the idea from becoming set, and all the while experimenting with various different formulations. And by means of many trials I would recapture that pure sensation and confirm its nature—much as a dog, attracted by the basic aroma of good food given off by a bone, prolongs the spell it is under by playing with the bone.

For me, the attempts at rephrasing took the form of boxing and fencing, about which I will say more later. It was natural that my rephrasing of the pure sense of strength should turn in the direction of the flash of the fist and the stroke of the bamboo sword; for that which lay at the end of the flashing fist, and beyond the blow of the bamboo sword, was precisely what constituted the most certain proof of that invisible light given off by the muscles. It was an attempt to reach the "ultimate sensation" that lies just a hairsbreadth beyond the reach of the senses.

Something, I felt sure, lurked in the empty space that lay there. Even with the aid of that sense of pure power, it was possible only to reach a point one step this side of that thing; with the intellect, or with artistic intuition, it was not even possible to get within ten or twenty paces. Art, admittedly, could probably give "expression" to it in some form or other. Yet "expression" requires a medium; in my case, it seemed, the abstract function of the words that would serve as the medium had the effect of being a barrier to everything else. And it seemed unlikely that the act of expression would satisfy one who had been motivated at the outset by doubts about that very act.

It is not surprising that an anathema for words should draw one's attention to the essentially dubious nature of the act of expression. Why do we conceive the desire to give expression to things that cannot be said—and sometimes succeed? Such success is a phenomenon that occurs when a subtle arrangement of words excites the reader's imagination to an extreme degree; at that moment, author and reader become accomplices in a crime of the imagination. And when their complicity gives rise to a work of literature—that "thing that is not a thing"—people call it "creation" and inquire no further.

In actual fact, words, armed with their abstract function, originally put in their appearance as a working of the logos designed to bring order to the chaos of the world of concrete objects, and expression was essentially an attempt to turn the abstract functioning back on itself and, like an electric current that flows in reverse, summon up a world of phenomena with the aid of words alone. It was in accordance with this idea that I suggested earlier that all works of literature were a kind of beautiful transformation of language. "Expression," by its very function, means the recreation of a world of concrete objects using language alone.

How many lazy men's truths have been admitted in the name of imagination! How often has the term imagination been used to prettify the unhealthy tendency of the soul to soar off in a boundless quest after truth, leaving the body where it always was! How often have men escaped from the pains of their own bodies with the aid of that sentimental aspect of the imagination that feels the ills of others' flesh as its own! And how often has the imagination unquestioningly exalted spiritual sufferings whose relative value was in fact excessively difficult to gauge! And when this type of arrogance of the imagination links together the artist's act of expression and its accomplices, there comes into existence a kind of fictional "thing"—the work of art—and it is this interference from a large number of such "things" that has steadily perverted and altered reality. As a result, men end up by coming into contact only with shadows and lose the courage to make themselves at home with the tribulations of their own flesh.

That which lurked beyond the flash of the fist and the stroke of the fencing sword was at the opposite pole from verbal expression—that much, at least, was apparent from the feeling it conveyed of being the essence of something extremely concrete, the essence, even, of reality. In no sense at all could it be called "a shadow." Beyond the fist, beyond the tip of the bamboo sword, a new reality had reared its head, a reality that rejected all attempts to make it abstract—indeed, that flatly rejected all expression of phenomena by resort to abstractions.

There, above all, lay the essence of action and of power. That reality, in popular parlance, was referred to quite simply as "the opponent."

The opponent and I dwelt in the same world. When I looked, the opponent was seen; when the opponent looked, I was seen; we faced each other, moreover, without any intermediary imagination, both belonging to the same world of action and strength—the world, that is, of "being seen." The opponent was in no sense an idea, for although by climbing step by step up the ladder of verbal expression in pursuit of an idea, and by gazing intently at that idea, we may well succeed in blinding ourselves to the light, that idea will never gaze back at us. In a realm where at every moment one's gaze is returned, one is never given time to express things in words. In order to express oneself, one needs to stand outside the world in question. Since that world as a whole never returns one's scrutiny, one is given time to look, and to express at leisure what one has found. But one will never succeed in getting at the essence of a reality that returns one's gaze.

It was the opponent—the opponent that lurked in the empty space beyond the flash of the fist and the blow of the fencing sword, gazing back at one—that constituted the true essence of things. Ideas do not stare back; things do. Beyond verbal expressions, ideas can be seen flitting behind the semitransparency of the fictional things they have achieved. Beyond action, one may glimpse, flitting behind the semitransparent space it has achieved (the opponent), the "thing." To the man of action, that "thing" appears as death, which bears down on him—the great black bull of the toreador—without any agency of the imagination.

Even so, I could not bring myself to believe in it except when it appeared at the very extremity of consciousness; I had perceived dimly, too, that the only physical proof of the existence of consciousness was suffering. Beyond doubt, there was a certain splendor in pain, which bore a deep affinity to the splendor that lies hidden within strength.

It is common experience that no technique of action can become effective until repeated practice has drummed it into the unconscious areas of the mind. What I was interested in, however, was something slightly different. On the one hand, my desire to have pure experience of consciousness was staked on the body-strength-action series, while on the other hand my passion for pure experience was staked on the given moment when, thanks to the reflex action of the pretrained subconscious, the body put forth its highest skill. And the only thing that truly attracted me was the point at which these two mutually opposed attempts coincided—the point of contact, in other words, at which the absolute value of consciousness and the absolute value of the body fitted exactly into each other.

The befuddling of the wits by means of drugs or alcohol was not, of course, my aim. My only interest lay in following consciousness through to its extreme limits, so as to discover at what point it was converted into unconscious power. That being so, what surer witness to the persistence of consciousness to its outer limits could I have found than physical suffering? There is an undeniable interdependence between consciousness and physical suffering, and consciousness, conversely, affords the surest possible proof of the persistence of bodily distress.

Pain, I came to feel, might well prove to be the sole proof of the persistence of consciousness within the flesh, the sole physical expression of consciousness. As my body acquired muscle, and in turn strength, there was gradually born within me a tendency towards the positive acceptance of pain, and my interest in physical suffering deepened. Even so, I would not have it believed that this development was a result of the workings of my imagination. My discovery was made directly, with my body, thanks to the sun and the steel.

As many people must have experienced for themselves, the greater the accuracy of a blow from a boxing glove or a fencing sword, the more it is felt as a counterblow rather than as a direct assault on the opponent's person. One's own blow, one's own strength, creates a kind of hollow. A blow is successful if, at that instant, the opponent's body fits into that hollow in space and assumes a form precisely identical with it.

How is it that a blow can be experienced in such a way; what makes a blow successful? Success comes when both the timing and placing of the blow are just right. But more than this, it happens when the choice of time and target—one's judgement—manages to catch the foe momentarily off guard, when one has an intuitive apprehension of that off-guard moment a fraction of a second *before* it becomes perceptible to the senses. This apprehension is a quantity that is unknowable even to the self and is acquired through a process of long training. By the time the right moment is consciously perceptible, it is already too late. It is too late, in other words, when that which lurks in the space beyond the flashing fist and the tip of the sword has taken shape. By the moment it takes shape, it must already be snugly ensconced in that hollow in space that one has marked out and created. It is at this instant that victory in the fray is born.

At the height of the fray, I found, the tardy process of creating muscle, whereby strength creates form and form creates strength, is repeated so swiftly that it becomes imperceptible to the eye. Strength, that like light emitted its own rays, was constantly renewed, destroying and creating form as it went. I saw for myself how the form that was beautiful and fitting overcame the form that was ugly and imprecise. Its distortion invariably implied an opening for the foe and a blurring of the rays of strength.

The defeat of the foe occurs when he accommodates his form to the hollow in space that one has already marked out; at that moment, one's own form must preserve a constant precision and beauty. And the form itself must have an extreme adaptability, a matchless flexibility, so that it resembles a series of sculptures created from moment to moment by a fluid body. The continuous radiation of strength must create its own shape, just as a continuous jet of water will maintain the shape of a fountain.

Surely, I felt, the tempering by sun and steel to which I submitted over such a long period was none other than a process of creating this kind of fluid sculpture. And insofar as the body thus fashioned belonged strictly to life, its whole value, I came to feel, must lie in that moment-to-moment splendor. That, indeed, is the reason why human sculpture has striven so hard to commemorate the momentary glory of the flesh in imperishable marble.

It followed that death lay only a short way beyond that particular moment.

Here, I felt, I was gaining a clue to an inner understanding of the cult of the hero. The cynicism that regards all hero worship as comical is always shadowed by a sense of physical inferiority. Invariably, it is the man who believes himself to be physically lacking in heroic attributes who speaks mockingly of the hero; and when he does so, how dishonest it is that his phraseology, partaking ostensibly of a logic so universal and general, should not (or at least should be assumed by the general public not to) give any clue to his physical characteristics. I have yet to hear hero worship mocked by a man endowed with what might justly be called heroic physical attributes. Facile cynicism, invariably, is related to feeble muscles or obesity, while the cult of the hero and a mighty nihilism are always related to a mighty body and well-tempered muscles. For the cult of the hero is, ultimately, the basic principle of the body, and in the long run is intimately involved with the contrast between the robustness of the body and the destruction that is death.

The body carries quite sufficient persuasion to destroy the comic aura that surrounds an excessive self-awareness; for though a fine body may be tragic, there is in it no trace of the comic. The thing that ultimately saves the flesh from being ridiculous is the element of death that resides in the healthy, vigorous body; it is this, I realized, that sustains the dignity of the flesh. How comic would one find the gaiety and elegance of the bullfighter were his trade entirely divorced from associations of death!

Nevertheless, whenever one sought after the ultimate sensation, the moment of victory was always an insipid sensation. Ultimately, the opponent—the "reality that stares back at one"—is death. Since death, it seems, will yield to no one, the glory of victory can be nothing more than a purely worldly glory in its highest form. And if it is only a worldly glory, I told myself, then one ought to be able to secure something very similar to it by resorting to the verbal arts.

Yet the thing that we sense in the finest sculpture—as in the bronze charioteer of Delphi, where the glory, the pride, and the shyness reflected in the moment of victory are given faithful immortality—is the swift approach of the spectre of death just on the other side of the victor. At the same time, by showing us symbolically the limits of spatiality in the art of sculpture, it intimates that nothing but decline lies beyond the greatest human glory. The sculptor, in his arrogance, has sought to capture life only at its supreme moment.

If the solemnity and dignity of the body arise solely from the element of mortality that lurks within it, then the road that leads to death, I reasoned, must have some private path connecting with pain, suffering, and the continuing consciousness that is proof of life. And I could not help feeling that if there were some incident in which violent death pangs and well-developed muscles were skillfully combined, it could only occur in response to the aesthetic demands of destiny. Not, of course, that destiny often lends an ear to aesthetic considerations.

Even in my boyhood, I was not unfamiliar with various types of physical distress, but the addled brains and oversensitivity of adolescence confused them hopelessly with spiritual suffering. As a middle-school boy, a forced march from Gora to Sengoku-bara, then over Otome Pass to the plain at the foot of Mt. Fuji, was an undoubted trial, but all I extracted from my tribulations was a passive, mental type of suffering. I lacked the physical courage to seek out suffering for myself, to take pain unto myself.

The acceptance of suffering as a proof of courage was the theme of primitive initiation rites in the distant past, and all such rites were at the same time ceremonies of death and resurrection. Men have by now forgotten the profound hidden struggle between consciousness and the body that exists in courage, and physical courage in particular. Consciousness is generally considered to be passive, and the active body to constitute the essence of all that is bold and daring; yet in the drama of physical courage the roles are, in fact, reversed. The flesh beats a steady retreat into its function of self-defense, while it is clear consciousness that controls the decision that sends the body soaring into self-abandonment. It is the ultimate in clarity of consciousness that constitutes one of the strongest contributing factors in self-abandonment.

To embrace suffering is the constant role of physical courage; and physical courage is, as it were, the source of that taste for understanding and appreciating death that, more than anything else, is a prime condition for making true awareness of death possible. However much the closeted philosopher mulls over the idea of death, so long as he remains divorced from the physical courage that is a prerequisite for an awareness of it, he will remain unable even to begin to grasp it. I must make it clear that I am talking of "physical" courage; the "conscience of the intellectual" and "intellectual courage" are no concern of mine here.

Nevertheless, the fact remains that I was living in an age when the fencing sword was no longer a direct symbol of the real sword, and the real sword in sword-play sliced through nothing but air. The art of fencing was a summation of every type of manly beauty; yet, insofar as that manliness was no longer of any practical use in society, it was scarcely distinguishable from art that depended solely on the imagination. Imagination

I detested. For me, fencing ought to be something that admitted of no intervention by the imagination.

The cynics—well aware that there is nobody who despises the imagination so thoroughly as the dreamer, whose dreams are a process of the imagination—will, I am sure, scoff at my confession in their own minds.

Yet my dreams became, at some stage, my muscles. The muscles that I had made, that existed, might give scope for the imagination of others, but no longer admitted of being gnawed away by my own imagination. I had reached a stage where I was rapidly making acquaintance with the world of those who are "seen."

If it was a special property of muscles that they fed the imagination of others while remaining totally devoid of imagination themselves, then in fencing I was seeking to go one step further and achieve pure action that admitted of no imagination, either by the self or by others. Sometimes it seemed that my wish had been fulfilled, at others that it had not. Yet either way, it was physical strength that fought, that ran fleet of foot, that cried aloud. . . .

How did the groups of muscles, normally so heavy, so dark, so unchangingly static, know the moment of white-hot frenzy in action? I loved the freshness of the consciousness that rippled unceasingly beneath spiritual tension, whatever kind it might be. I could no longer believe that it was purely an intellectual quality of my own that the copper of excitement should be lined with the silver of awareness. It was this that made frenzy what it was. For I had begun to believe that it was the muscles—powerful, statically so well organized and so silent—that were the true source of the clarity of my consciousness. The occasional pain in the muscles of a blow that missed the shield gave rise instantly to a still tougher consciousness that suppressed the pain, and imminent shortage of breath gave rise to a frenzy that conquered it. Thus I glimpsed from time to time another sun quite different from that by which I had been so long blessed, a sun full of the fierce dark flames of feeling, a sun of death that would never burn the skin yet gave forth a still stranger glow.

This second sun was essentially far more dangerous to the intellect than the first sun had ever been. It was this danger more than anything else that delighted me.

What, now, of my dealings with words during this same period? By now, I had made of my style something appropriate to my muscles: it had become flexible and free; all fatty embellishment had been stripped from it, while "muscular" ornament—ornament, that is, that though possibly without use in modern civilization was still as necessary as ever for purposes of prestige and presentability—had been assiduously maintained. I disliked a style that was merely functional as much as one that was merely sensuous.

Nevertheless, I was on an isolated island of my own. Just as my body was isolated, so my style was on the verge of non-communication; it was a style that did not accept, but rejected. More than anything, I was preoccupied with distinction (not that my own style necessarily had it). My ideal style would have had the grave beauty of polished wood in the entrance hall of a samurai mansion on a winter's day.

In my style, as hardly needs pointing out, I progressively turned my back on the preferences of the age. Abounding in antitheses, clothed in an old-fashioned, weighty solemnity, it did not lack nobility of a kind; but it maintained the same ceremonial, grave pace wherever it went, marching through other people's bedrooms with precisely the same tread as elsewhere. Like some military gentleman, it went about with chest out and shoulders back, despising other men's styles for the way they stooped, sagged at the knees, even —heaven forbid!— swayed at the hips.

I knew, of course, that there are some truths in this world that one cannot see unless one unbends one's posture. But such things could well be left to others.

Somewhere within me, I was beginning to plan a union of art and life, of style and the ethos of action. If style was similar to muscles and patterns of behavior, then its function was obviously to restrain the wayward imagination. Any truths that might be overlooked as a result were no concern of mine. Nor did I care one jot that the fear and horror of confusion and ambiguity eluded my style. I had made up my mind that I would select only one particular truth, and avoid aiming at any all-inclusive truth. Enervating, ugly truths I ignored;

by means of a process of diplomatic selection within the spirit, I sought to avoid the morbid influence exerted on men by indulgence in the imagination. Nevertheless, it was dangerous, obviously, to understimate or ignore its influence. There was no telling when the sickly forces of an invisible imagination, still lying in wait, might launch their cowardly assault from without the carefully arrayed fortifications of style. Day and night, I stood guard on the ramparts. Occasionally, something—a red fire—would flare up like a signal on the dark plain stretching endlessly into the night before me. I would try to tell myself that it was a bonfire. Then, as suddenly as it had appeared, the fire would vanish again. As guard and weapon against imagination and its henchman sensibility, I had style. The tension of the all-night watch, whether by land or by sea, was what I sought after in my style. More than anything, I detested defeat. Can there be any worse defeat than when one is corroded and seared from within by the acid secretions of sensibility until finally one loses one's outline, dissolves, liquefies; or when the same thing happens to the society about one, and one alters one's own style to match it?

Everyone knows that masterpieces, ironically enough, sometimes arise from the midst of such defeat, from the death of the spirit. Though I might retreat a pace and admit such masterpieces as victories, I knew that they were victories without a struggle, battleless victories of a kind peculiar to art. What I sought was the struggle as such, whichever way it might go. I had no taste for defeat

—much less victory—without a fight. At the same time, I knew only too well the deceitful nature of any kind of conflict in art. If I must have a struggle, I felt I should take the offensive in fields outside art; in art, I should defend my citadel. It was necessary to be a sturdy defender within art, and a good fighter outside it. The goal of my life was to acquire all the various attributes of the warrior.

During the postwar period, when all accepted values were upset, I often thought and remarked to others that now if ever was the time for reviving the old Japanese ideal of a combination of letters and the martial arts, of art and action. For a while after that, my interest strayed from that particular ideal; then, as I gradually learned from the sun and the steel the secret of how to pursue words with the body (and not merely pursue the body with words), the two poles within me began to maintain a balance, and the generator of my mind, so to speak, switched from a direct to an alternating current. My mind devised a system that by installing within the self two mutually antipathetic elements—two elements that flowed alternately in opposite directions—gave the appearance of inducing an ever wider split in the personality, yet in practice created at each moment a living balance that was constantly being destroyed and brought back to life again. The embracing of a dual polarity within the self and the acceptance of contradiction and collision—such was my own blend of "art and action."

In this way, it seemed to me, my long-standing interest in the opposite of the literary principle began for the first time to bear fruit. The principle of the sword, it seemed, lay in its allying death not with pessimism and impotence but with abounding energy, the flower of physical perfection, and the will to fight. Nothing could be farther removed from the principle of literature. In literature, death is held in check yet at the same time used as a driving force; strength is devoted to the construction of empty fictions; life is held in reserve, blended to just the right degree with death, treated with preservatives, and lavished on the production of works of art that possess a weird eternal life. Action—one might say—perishes with the blossom; literature is an imperishable flower. And an imperishable flower, of course, is an artificial flower.

Thus to combine action and art is to combine the flower that wilts and the flower that lasts forever, to blend within one individual the two most contradictory desires in humanity, and the respective dreams of those desires' realization. What, then, occurs as a result?

To be utterly familiar with the essence of these two things—of which one must be false if the other is true—and to know completely their sources and partake of their mysteries, is secretly to destroy the ultimate dreams of one concerning the other. When action views itself as reality and art as falsehood, it entrusts this falsehood with authority for giving final endorsement to its own truth and, hoping to take advantage of the falsehood, sets it in charge of its dreams. It is thus that epic poems came to be written. On the other hand, when art considers itself as the reality and action as the falsehood, it once more envisages that falsehood as the peak of its own ultimate fictional world; it has been forced to realize that its own death is no longer backed up by the falsehood, that hard on the heels of the reality of its own work came the reality of death. This death is a fearful death, the death that descends on the human being who has never lived; yet he can at least dream, ultimately, of the existence in the world of action—the falsehood—of a death that is other than his own.

By the destruction of these ultimate dreams I mean the perception of two hidden truths: that the flower of falsehood dreamed of by the man of action is no more than an artificial flower; and, on the other hand, that the death bolstered up by falsehood of which art dreams in no way confers any special favors. In short, the dual approach cuts one off from all salvation by dreams: the two secrets that should never by rights have been brought face to face see through each other. Within one body, and without flinching, the collapse of the ultimate principles of life and of death must be accepted.

One may well ask if it is possible for anyone to live this duality in practice. Fortunately, it is extremely rare for the duality to assume its absolute form; it is the kind of ideal that, if realized, would be over in a moment. For the secret of this inwardly conflicting, ultimate duality is that, though it may make itself constantly foreseen in the form of a vague apprehension, it will never be put to the test until the moment of death. Then—at the very moment when the dual ideal that offers no salvation is about to be realized—the person who is preoccupied with this duality will betray that ideal from one side or the other. Since it was life that bound him to the ruthless perception of that ideal, he will betray that perception once he finds himself face to face with death. Otherwise, death for him would be unbearable.

As long as we are alive, however, we may dally with any type of outlook we choose, a fact that is borne out by the constant deaths in sport and the refreshing re-births that follow. Victory where the mind is concerned comes from the balance that is achieved in the face of ever-imminent destruction.

Since my own mind was forever beset by boredom, all but the most difficult, virtually impossible tasks failed by now to arouse its interest. More specifically, it was no longer interested in anything save the dangerous type of game in which the mind put itself in peril—in the game, and in the refreshing "shower" that followed.

At one time, one of the aims of my mind was to know how the man with a massive physique felt about the world around him. This was obviously a problem too great for mere knowledge to handle, for though knowledge may penetrate the darkness by using the many creeping vines of sensation and intuition as guide ropes, here the vines themselves were uprooted; the source that sought to know belonged to me, while the right to the inclusive sense of existence was granted to the other side.

A little thought will make this clear. The sense of existence of a man with a massive physique must, in itself, be of the kind that embraces the whole world; for that man, considered as a object of knowledge, everything outside himself (including me) must necessarily be transferred onto the objective outside world experienced by his senses. No accurate picture can be grasped under such circumstances unless one responds with a still more embracing awareness. It is like trying to know how the native of another country experiences existence; in such a case, all we can do is to apply inclusive, abstract concepts such as mankind, universal humanity, and so on, and to make deductions using these hypothetical yardsticks. This, however, is not an exact knowledge, but a method that leaves the ultimately unknowable elements untouched and deduces by analogy with the other, shared elements. The real question is staved off; the things one "really wants to know" are shelved. The only other alternative is for the imagination to take over unashamedly and adorn the other side with a whole variety of poems and fantasies.

For me, however, all fantasy suddenly vanished. My bored mind had been chasing after the unintelligible when, abruptly, the mystery disintegrated . . . Suddenly, it was I who had a fine physique.

Thus, those who had been on the other side of the stream were here, on the same side as myself. The riddle had gone; death remained the only mystery. And since this freedom from riddles had been in no way a product of the mind, the latter's pride was terribly hurt. Somewhat defiantly, it began to yawn once more, once more began to sell itself to the detested imagination, and the only thing that belonged eternally to the imagination was death.

Yet, where is the difference? If the deepest sources of the morbid imagination that falls on one by night —of the voluptuous imagination, inducer of sensual abandon—lie, one and all, in death, how does *that* death differ from the glorious death? What distinguishes the heroic from the decadent death? The dual way's cruel withholding of salvation proves that they are ultimately the same, and that the literary ethic and the ethic of action are no more than pathetic efforts of resistance against death and oblivion.

What difference there might be resolves itself into the presence or absence of the idea of honor, which regards death as "something to be seen," and the presence or absence of the formal aesthetic of death that goes with it—in other words, the tragic nature of the approach to death and the beauty of the body going to its doom. Thus, where a beautiful death is concerned, men are condemned to inequalities and degrees of fortune commensurate with the inequalities and degrees of fortune bestowed on them by fate at their birth—though this inequality is obscured nowadays by the fact that modern man is almost devoid of the desire of the ancient Greeks to live "beautifully" and die "beautifully."

Why should a man be associated with beauty only through a heroic, violent death? In ordinary life, society maintains a careful surveillance to ensure that men shall have no part in beauty; physical beauty in the male, when considered as an "object" in itself without any intermediate agent, is despised, and the profession of the male actor—which involves constantly being "seen"—is far from being accorded true respect. A strict rule is imposed where men are concerned. It is this: a man must under normal circumstances never permit his own objectivization; he can only be objectified through the supreme action—which is, I suppose, the moment of death, the moment when, even without being seen, the fiction of being seen and the beauty of the object are permitted. Of such is the beauty of the suicide squad, which is recognized as beauty not only in the spiritual sense but, by men in general, in an ultra-erotic sense also. Moreover, serving as agent in this case is a heroic action of an intensity beyond the resources of the ordinary mortal, so that "objectivization" without an agent is not possible here. However close mere words may get to this moment of supreme action that acts as intermediary for beauty, they can no more overtake it than a flying body can attain the speed of light.

But what I was trying to describe here was not beauty. To discuss beauty is to discuss the question "in depth." This was not my intention: what I sought to do was to arrange a great variety of ideas like dice of hard ivory and to set limits to the function of each.

I discovered, then, that the profoundest depths of the imagination lay in death. It is natural, perhaps, that quite apart from the necessity to prepare defenses against the encroachments of the imagination, I should have conceived the idea of turning the imagination that had so long tormented me back on itself, changing it into something that I could use as a weapon for counterattack. However, where art as such was concerned, my style had already built forts here, there, and everywhere, and was successfully holding the encroachments of the imagination in check. If I was to plan such a counterattack, it must take place in some field outside that of art. It was this, more than anything else, that first drew me towards the idea of the martial arts.

At one time, I had been the type of boy who leaned at the window, forever watching out for unexpected events to come crowding in towards him. Though I might be unable to change the world myself, I could not but hope that the world would change of its own accord. As that kind of boy, with all the accompanying anxieties, the transformation of the world was an urgent necessity for me; it nourished me from day to day; it was something without which I could not have lived. The idea of the changing of the world was as much a necessity as sleep and three meals a day. It was the womb that nourished my imagination.

What followed in practice was in one sense a transformation of the world, in another it was not. Even though the world might change into the kind I hoped for, it lost its rich charm at the very instant of change. The thing that lay at the far end of my dreams was extreme danger and destruction; never once had I envisaged happiness. The most appropriate type of daily life for me was a day-by-day world destruction; peace was the most difficult and abnormal state to live in.

Unfortunately, I lacked the physical wherewithal to cope with this. Wearing upon my sleeve a susceptibility that knew no way of resistance, I watched out for the unexpected, telling myself that when it came I would accept it rather than struggle with it.

Much later, I realized that if the psychological life of this excessively decadent youth had happened to be backed up by strength and the will to fight, it would have constituted a perfect analogy with the life of the warrior. It was an oddly exhilarating discovery. In making it, I put within my grasp the opportunity to turn the imagination back on itself.

If the only natural world for me was one in which death was an everyday, self-evident matter, and if what was natural to me was very easily attainable, not through artificial devices, but by means of perfectly unoriginal concepts of duty, then nothing could be more natural than that I should gradually succumb to temptation and seek to replace imagination by duty. No moment is so dazzling as when everyday imaginings concerning death and danger and world destruction are transformed into duty. To do this, however, required the nurturing of the body, of the strength and will to fight, and the techniques to fight with. Their development could be entrusted to the same type of methods as had once served to develop the imagination; for were not the imagination and swordmanship the same insofar as they were techniques nurtured by a familiarity with death? Both were techniques, moreover, that led one closer and closer towards destruction the more sensitive they became.

I now realize that the kind of task in which to burnish the imagination for death and danger comes to have the same significance as burnishing the sword, had long been calling to me from a distance; only weakness and cowardice had made me avoid it.

To keep death in mind from day to day, to focus each moment upon inevitable death, to make sure one's worst forebodings coincided with one's dreams of glory . . . if that was all, then it was sufficient to transfer to the world of the flesh what I had long been doing in the world of the spirit.

I have already written of how assiduously I was making preparations for accepting such a wrenching change, getting myself ready to accept it at any time. The theory that anything could be recovered had come into being within me. As it had become clear that even the body— ostensibly the prisoner of time in its moment-to-moment growth and decline—could be recovered, then it was not odd that I should conceive the idea of time itself as recoverable.

For me, the idea that time was recoverable meant that the beautiful death that had earlier eluded me had also become possible. What was more, during the past ten years I had learned strength, I had learned suffering, battle, and self-conquest; I had learned the courage to accept them all with joy.

I was beginning to dream of my capabilities as a fighting man.

. . . It is a rather risky matter to discuss a happiness that has no need of words.

The one thing I am sure can easily be deduced from what I have written is that in order to bring about what I refer to here as happiness, an extremely troublesome set of conditions must first be fulfilled, and an extremely complex set of procedures gone through.

The short period—one month and a half—of army life that I later experienced yielded many glittering fragments of happiness, but there is one of them—an unforgettable, all-embracing sense of happiness that I experienced at a moment in itself apparently quite insignificant and quite unmilitary—that I feel compelled to write of here. Although I was in the midst of a group army life, this supreme sense of wellbeing came upon me, as on every previous occasion in my life, when I was quite alone.

It happened at dusk on May 25, a beautiful day in early summer. I was attached to a parachute squad; the day's training was over; I had been for a bath, and was on my way back to the dormitory.

The late afternoon sky was dyed in shades of blue and pink, and the turf spread below was an even, glowing jade. Here and there on either side of the path along which

I walked stood the ageing, robust, wooden buildings, nostalgic souvenirs of an age when this had been the cavalry school: the covered riding paddock, now a gymnasium, the stables, now a post-exchange. . . .

I was still in my P.T. clothes: long white cotton training pants just issued that day, rubber gym shoes, a running shirt. Even the mud that already soiled the bottom of the pants contributed to my sense of wellbeing.

That morning's training in handling a parachute, the extraordinarily rarified feeling as for the first time one committed oneself to the empty air, still lingered inside me, a transparent residue, fragile as a medicinal wafer. The deep, rapid breathing caused by the circuit training and running that followed had pervaded my whole body with a pleasing lethargy. Rifles, weapons of every kind, were at hand. My shoulder was ready for slinging a gun at any time. I had run to my heart's content over the green grass, felt the sun burning my skin a golden brown; beneath the summer sunlight, I had seen, thirty-five feet below me, people's shadows sharply etched and firmly attached to their feet. I had jumped into space from the summit of the silver tower, aware as I went of how the shadow that I myself would cast among them the next instant would lie isolated like a black puddle on the earth, untied to my body. At that moment I was, beyond all doubt, freed from my shadow, from my self-awareness.

My day had been full to the brim of the body and of action. There was physical excitement, and strength, and sweat, and muscle; the green grass of summer was everywhere, a breeze stirred the dust on the path I walked along, the sun's rays slowly slanted ever more obliquely, and in my training pants and gym shoes I walked amidst them quite naturally. Here was the life I had wanted. At that time, I savored the same solitary, rough-and-ready joy of the physical training instructor walking back between the old school building and the shrubbery after losing himself in the beauty of physical training on a summer's evening.

I sensed in it an absolute rest for the spirit, a beatification of the flesh. Summer, white clouds, the empty blue of the sky following the final lesson of the day, and the touch of nostaligic sadness tinging the glitter of sunlight filtering through the trees, induced a sense of intoxication. I existed. . . .

How complex were the procedures necessary to attain this existence! Within it, a large number of concepts that for me were close to fetishes achieved direct association with my body and senses, quite independently of the agency of words. The army, physical training, summer, clouds, sunset, the green of summer grasses, the white training suit, sweat, muscle, and just the faintest whiff of death. . . . Nothing was lacking; every piece of the mosaic was in place. I had absolutely no need of any others, and thus no need of words. The world I was in was made up of conceptual elements that were as pure as angels; all foreign elements had been temporarily swept aside, and I overflowed with the infinite joy of being one with the world, a joy akin to that produced by cold water on skin warmed by the summer sun.

. . . Quite possibly, what I call happiness may coincide with what others call the moment of imminent danger. For that world into which I blended without the medium of words, filling myself thereby with a sense of happiness, was none other than the tragic world. The tragedy, of course, was at that moment still unfulfilled; yet all the seeds of tragedy were within it; ruin was implicit in it; it lacked entirely any "future." Obviously, the basis of my happiness was the joy of having completely acquired the qualifications necessary to dwell therein. The basis of my pride was the feeling that I had acquired this precious passport, not through words, but through the cultivation of the body and that alone. This world that was the only place where I could breathe freely, that was so utterly remote from the commonplace and lacking in future—this world I had pursued unceasingly, ever since the war had ended, with a burning sense of frustration. But words had played no part in giving it to me; on the contrary, they had spurred me on ever farther and farther from it: for even the most destructive verbal expression was but an integral part of the artist's daily task.

How ironical it was! At a period when the futureless cup of catastrophe had been brimming over, I had not been given the qualifications for drinking from it. I had gone away, and when, after long training, I had returned armed with those qualifications in fullest measure, it was to find the cup drained, its bottom coldly visible, and myself past forty. Unfortunately, moreover, the only liquid that might quench my thirst was that which others had drained before me.

Everything was not, as I had deluded myself, recoverable. Time was beyond recall after all. And yet, as I now realized, the attempt to fly in the face of the relentless march of time was perhaps the most characteristic feature of the way in which, since the war, I had sought to live by committing every possible heresy. If, as was commonly believed, time was indeed irreversible, was it possible that I should be living here in this way? I had, indeed, good reason within myself to pose this question.

Refusing utterly to recognize the conditions of my own existence, I had set about acquiring a different existence instead. Insofar as words, by endorsing my existence, had laid down the conditions for that existence, the steps it was necessary to take to acquire another existence involved flinging myself bodily on the side of the phantom evoked and radiated by words; it meant changing from a being that created words to one that was created by words; it meant, quite simply, using subtle and elaborate procedures in order to secure the momentary shadow of existence. It was logical, indeed, that I should have succeeded in existing only at one solitary, selected moment of my short army life. The basis of my happiness, obviously, lay in my having transformed myself, albeit for only a moment, into a phantom formed by the shadows cast by far-off, moldering words from the past. By now, though, it was not words that endorsed my existence. This type of existence that derived from rejecting the endorsement of existence by words, had to be endorsed by something different. That "something different" was muscle.

The sense of existence that produced such an intense happiness disintegrated, of course, a moment later, but the muscles miraculously survived the disintegration. Unfortunately, however, a mere sense of existence is not enough to make one perceive that the muscles have escaped dissolution; one needs to afford proof of one's muscles with one's own eyes, and seeing is the antithesis of existing.

The subtle contradiction between self-awareness and existence began to trouble me.

I reasoned that if one wants to identify seeing and existing, the nature of the self-awareness should be made as centripetal as possible. If only one can direct the eye of self-awareness so intently towards the interior and the self that self-awareness forgets the outer forms of existence, then one can "exist" as surely as the "I" in Amiel's *Diary*. But this existence is of an odd kind, like a transparent apple whose core is fully visible from the outside; and the only endorsement of such existence lies in words. It is the classical type of existence experienced by the solitary, humanistic man of letters. . . .

But one also comes across a type of self-awareness that concerns itself exclusively with the form of things. For this type of self-awareness, the antinomy between seeing and existing is decisive, since it involves the question of how the core of the apple can be seen through the ordinary, red, opaque skin, and also how the eye that looks at that glossy red apple from the outside can penetrate into the apple and itself become the core. The apple in this case, moreover, must have a perfectly ordinary existence, its color a healthy red.

To continue the metaphor, let us picture a single, healthy apple. This apple was not called into existence by words, nor is it possible that the core should be completely visible from the outside like Amiel's peculiar fruit. The inside of the apple is naturally quite invisible. Thus at the heart of that apple, shut up within the flesh of the fruit, the core lurks in its wan darkness, tremblingly anxious to find some way to reassure itself that it is a perfect apple. The apple certainly exists, but to the core this existence as yet seems inadequate; if words cannot endorse it, then the only way to endorse it is with the eyes. Indeed, for the core the only sure mode of existence is to exist and to see at the same time. There is only one method of solving this contradiction. It is for a knife to be plunged deep into the apple so that it is split open and the core is exposed to the light—to the same light, that is, as the surface skin. Yet then the existence of the cut apple falls into fragments; the core of the apple sacrifices existence for the sake of seeing.

When I realized that the perfect sense of existence that disintegrated the very next moment could only be endorsed by muscle, and not by words, I was already personally enduring the fate that befell the apple. Admittedly, I could see my own muscles in the mirror. Yet seeing alone was not enough to bring me into contact with the basic roots of my sense of existence, and an immeasurable distance remained between me and the euphoric sense of pure being. Unless I rapidly closed that distance, there was little hope of bringing that sense of existence to life again. In other words, the self-awareness that I staked on muscles could not be satisfied with the darkness of the pallid flesh pressing about it as an endorsement of its existence, but, like the blind core of the apple, was driven to crave certain proof of its existence so fiercely that it was bound, sooner or later, to destroy that existence. Oh, the fierce longing simply to see, without words!

The eye of self-awareness, used as it is to keeping a watch on the invisible self in an essentially centripetal fashion and via the good offices of words, does not place sufficient trust in visible things such as muscles. Inevitably, it addresses the muscles as follows:

"I admit you do not *seem* to be a illusion. But if so, I would like you to show how you function in order to live and move; show me your proper functions and how you fulfil your proper aims."

Thus the muscles start working in accordance with the demands of self-awareness; but in order to make the action exist unequivocally, a hypothetical enemy outside the muscles is necessary, and for the hypothetical enemy to make certain of its existence it must deal a blow to the realm of the senses fierce enough to silence the querulous complaints of self-awareness. That, precisely, is when the knife of the foe must come cutting into the flesh of the apple—or rather, the body. Blood flows, existence is destroyed, and the shattered senses give existence as a whole its first endorsement, closing the logical gap between seeing and existing. . . . And this is death.

In this way I learned that the momentary, happy sense of existence that I had experienced that summer sunset during my life with the army could be finally endorsed only by death.

All these things, of course, had been foreseen, and I knew too that the basic conditions for this made-to-order type of existence were none other than the "absolute" and the "tragic." Death began from the time when I set about acquiring an existence other than that of words. For however destructive a garb they might assume, words were deeply bound up with my instinct for survival, were a part of my very life. Was it not, essentially, when I first felt the desire to live that I began for the first time to use words effectively? It was words that would make me live on until I died a natural death; they were the slow-moving germs of a "sickness unto death."

I have written above of the affinity between my own illusions and those cherished by the warrior, and of my sympathy for the type of task in which burnishing the sword and burnishing the imagination for death and danger came to the same thing. This was something that made possible, through the agency of the flesh, every metaphor of the spiritual world. And everything, in fact, turned out just as expected.

Even so, the impression of enormous wasted effort that hangs about an army in peacetime oppressed me. Admittedly, this was due in large measure to the unfortunate nature of Japan's foundling army that deliberately keeps it far removed from any ideas of tradition or glory. Yet it reminded me of the repeated process of charging a vast battery that is eventually exhausted through normal leakage and has to be recharged; the power it generates is never used for any effective purpose. Everything is devoted to the enormous hypothesis of a "coming war." Training plans are drawn up in fine detail, the troops labor at their tasks, and the vacuum in which nothing happens progresses from day to day; bodies that were in peak condition yesterday have deteriorated ever so slightly today; old age is progressively cleared away, and youth replenished without intermission.

More clearly than ever before, I grasped the true efficacy of words. It is this void in the present progressive tense with which they deal. This void of the progressive, that may go on for ever while one waits for an absolute that may never come, is the true canvas on which words are painted. This can happen, moreover, because words, in marking the void, dye it as irrevocably as the gay colors and designs on Yuzen fabrics are fixed once they are rinsed in the clear waters of Kyoto's river, and in doing so consume the void completely moment by moment, becoming fixed in each instant, where they remain. Words are over as soon as they are spoken, as soon as they are written. Through the accumulation of these "endings," through the moment-to-moment rupture of life's sense of continuity, words acquire a certain power. At the very least, they diminish to some degree the overwhelming terror of the vast white walls in the waiting room where we await the arrival of the physician, the absolute. And in exchange for the way in which, by marking off each moment, they ceaselessly chop up life's sense of continuity, they act in a way that seems at least to translate the void into substance of a kind.

The power to "bring to an end"—even though this too may in itself be a fiction—is obviously present in words. The lengthy accounts written by prisoners in the condemned cell are a form of magic aimed at ending from moment to moment a long period of waiting that exceeds the limits of human endurance.

All we are left with is the freedom to choose which method we will try out when brought face to face with that void in the progressive tense, in the interval while we await the "absolute". Either way, we must make our preparations. That these preparations should be referred to as "spiritual development" is due to the desire that lurks to a greater or lesser extent in all human beings to fashion themselves, however unsuccessfully, in the image of the "absolute" to come. It is perhaps the most natural and decent of all desires, this wish that body and spirit alike should come to resemble the absolute.

Such a design, however, invariably ends in total failure. For however prolonged and intense the training, the body, inevitably, progresses little by little towards decay; however much one piles up verbal action, the spirit will not know the end. The spirit, having already lost its sense of the continuity of life as a result of the moment-to-moment ends imposed on it by words, can no longer distinguish a true end.

It is "time" that is responsible for this frustration and failure, yet very occasionally that same time confers a favor and rescues the project. Here lies the mysterious significance of an early death, which the Greeks envied as a sign of the love of the gods.

I, however, had already lost the morning face that belongs to youth alone—the face that, however deep it has sunk in the stagnant depths of fatigue the previous night, rises fresh and alive to breathe at the surface in the morning. In most people, alas, the unsophisticated habit of exposing the face, quite unconsciously, to the dazzling light of the morning persists to the end. The habit remains, the face changes. Before one realizes it, the true face is ravaged by anxiety and emotion; one does not perceive that it drags last night's fatigue like a heavy chain, nor does one realize the boorishness of exposing such a face to the sun. It is thus that men lose their manliness.

The reason is that once it has lost the natural brightness of youth, the manly face of the warrior must needs be a false face; it must be manufactured as a matter of policy. The army, I found, made this quite clear. The morning face presented by a commanding officer was a face for people to read things into, a face in which others might immediately find a criterion for the day's action. It was an optimistic face, designed to cover up the individual's private weariness and, no matter what despair he might be plunged into, to encourage others; it was thus a false face full of energy, spurning and shaking off the bad dreams of the previous night. And it was the only face with which men who lived too long could make obeisance to the morning sun.

In this respect, the face of the intellectual whose youth was past horrified me: it was ugly and impolitic. . . .

Having concerned myself from the outset of my literary life with methods for concealing rather than revealing myself, I marveled at the function of the uniform in the army. Just as the finest cloak of invisibility for words is muscle, so the finest cloak of invisibility for the body is the uniform. The military uniform, however, is made in such a way that it refuses to suit a scrawny body or a protruding belly.

The individuality as pared down by a uniform had, I found, an extraordinary simplicity and clearcut quality. In the eyes of others, the man who donned a uniform became thereby, quite simply, a combatant. Whatever his personality and private thoughts, whether he was a dreamer or a nihilist, whether magnanimous or parsimonious, however vast the gulf of sordidness that yawned beneath his uniform, however full he might be of vulgar ambition, he was still, quite simply, a combatant. Sooner or later, the uniform would be pierced by a bullet and stained with blood; in this respect, it matched remarkably well the special quality of muscles whereby self-endorsement inevitably meant self-destruction.

. . . For all that, though, I was in no sense a military man myself. The army is a profession that requires a great deal of technique. As I saw and noted well for myself, it demands, more than any other profession, a long period of careful training. In order not to lose the techniques once they are acquired, constant and unrelaxing practice is necessary, much as a pianist must practice every day in order not to lose his delicacy of touch.

Nothing gives the armed forces so much attraction as the fact that even the most trivial duty is ultimately an emanation of something far loftier and more glorious, and is linked, somewhere, with the idea of death. The man of letters, on the other hand, must scratch together his own glory from the rubbish within himself, already overfamiliar in every detail, and refurbish it for the public eye.

Two different voices constantly call to us. One comes from within, the other from without. The one from without is one's daily duty. If the part of the mind that responded to duty corresponded exactly with the voice from within, then one would indeed be supremely happy.

On a May afternoon of unseasonably cold drizzle, I was alone in the dormitory, the firing practice that I had been due to witness having been cancelled on account of the rain. It was chilly there on the plain skirting the foot of Mt. Fuji, more like a winter's day than early summer. On such a day, tall city buildings where men worked would be aglow with lights even in the daytime, and the women at home would be knitting by artificial light, or watching the television, perhaps repenting having put the gas fires away too soon. Ordinary bourgeois life held no force sufficiently compelling to drag one out into the chill drizzle without so much as an umbrella.

Unexpectedly, a non-commissioned officer arrived in a jeep to fetch me. The firing practice, he explained, was going ahead despite the rain.

The jeep drove steadily along the potholed road across the plain, lurching violently as it went.

Not a soul was in sight on the plain. The jeep climbed a slope down which the rain washed in sheets, and drove down the other side again. Visibility was restricted, the wind gathered strength, and the clumps of grass bowed down before it. From a gap in the hood, the cold rain beat mercilessly on my cheeks.

I was glad that they had come from the plain to fetch me on such a day. It was an emergency duty, a voice summoning me lustily from afar. The feeling of hastily leaving a warm lair in response to a voice calling from across the vast rain-blurred plain had a primitive appeal that I had not savored for many a day.

On such occasions, something unknown compels me, almost tears me away from the warm fireside. There is no reluctance or hesitation: I gladly go to meet the messenger from the ends of the earth (in most cases he has some connection with death or pleasure or instinct) and, in the instant of my departure, I abandon everything that is comfortable and familiar. I had, I felt, savored just such a moment long ago in the distant past.

In the past, though, the voice that had called me from without had not corresponded precisely to the voice from within. This, I believe, is because I was unable to meet the call from without with my body, managing barely to do so with words instead. I was familiar, it is true, with the sweet pain that occurred when it became entangled in the complex mesh of ideas, but I was ignorant as yet of the deep-rooted joy produced when the two types of summons, meeting in the body, find themselves perfectly matched.

Before long, there came the high-pitched whine of the guns, and I caught sight of the bright orange tracer shells being fired, with repeated corrections for error, at targets half obscured by the drifting rain. The next hour I spent sitting in the mire, with the rain beating down on me.

. . . I recall another memory.

I was running alone, one December 14, on the main track of the National Stadium beneath the first glimmerings of dawn. In reality, this kind of behavior was no more than a fictional "task"—a piece of drunken excess, one might well call it—yet I have never felt so keenly that I was enjoying the ultimate in extravagance, nor have I ever felt so sure that the daybreak belonged to me alone.

It was a freezing dawn. The National Stadium was a great lily of which the vast arena, utterly deserted, formed the overblown, speckled, greyish-white petals.

I wore only a running shirt and pants; the morning breeze struck chill to the bone; my hands were soon numb. As I passed the gloom in front of the stands on the east side, the cold was daunting; the west side, on which the first rays of the sun were already striking, was more bearable. I had circled the 400-meter track four times, and was on my fifth time round.

The sun peering over the top of the stands was still intercepted by the edge of the lily's petals, and the magenta of a reluctant dawn still lingered in the sky. The east side of the stadium, was touched by the last of the cold night-breeze.

As I ran, I breathed not only the knife-sharp air but the lingering aroma of the dawn. The tumult, the cries of joy from the stands, the smell of athlete's lotion heightened by the morning chill, the pounding of red hearts, the fierce resolve—of such was compounded the fragrance of that great lily, a fragrance that the stadium had retained all through the night. And the brick red of the track was, unmistakably, the color of the lily's pollen.

As I ran, my mind was filled with one idea: the

relationship between the voluptuous lily of dawn and the purity of the body.

So completely did this difficult metaphysical problem engross me that I went on running, oblivious to fatigue. It was a problem that, somewhere deep down, related to myself; it linked up with my boyhood hypocrisy concerning the purity and sanctity of the body; and it had its bearing, I suspected, on the distant martyrdom of Saint Sebastian.

The reader is asked to notice that I say nothing of my own everyday life. My intention is to talk only of the several mysteries to which I have been party.

Running, too, was a mystery. It immediately placed a non-routine burden on the heart, washing away the emotions of the daily round. Before long, my blood would not permit a halt of even a day or two. Something ceaselessly set me to work; my body could no longer tolerate indolence, but began instantly to thirst for violent action, forever urging me on. Thus for many a day I led a life that others might well dismiss as frenzied obsession. From the gymnasium to the fencing school, from the school to the gymnasium.... My solace lay more than anywhere—indeed lay solely—in the small rebirths that occurred immediately after exercise. Ceaseless motion, ceaseless violent deaths, ceaseless escape from cold objectivity—by now, I could no longer live without such mysteries. And—needless to say—within each mystery there lay a small imitation of death.

All unawares, I had embarked on a kind of pitiless

round. My age pursued me, murmuring behind my back "How long will it last?" Yet so firmly was I in the clutches of my healthy vice that to go back to the world of words without the mystery of these rebirths was no longer possible.

This does not imply, of course, that after my small rebirths of the soul and the flesh I went back reluctantly, with a sense of duty, to the world of words. On the contrary, this was the one procedure that ensured that I should return to them joyfully and with a glad heart.

The demands I made on words became still more strict and exacting. I shunned the latest styles like the plague. Perhaps I was gradually seeking to rediscover the unsullied fortress of words that I had known during the war.

It may be that I was trying to reconstruct everything according to the pattern that I had learned before, to find once more my fortress of words—that paradoxical base of freedom outside which I was forever threatened, yet inside which I enjoyed an unparalleled freedom.

It was also an attempt to recapture the intoxication I experienced, free from guilt about words, at that age when I asked words to fulfil only the purest of functions. And that meant trying to recover my own self as it had been when eaten away by the white ants of words, and to reinforce it with a sturdy body. It was an attempt to restore a state of affairs in which words (however far they might be from the truth) were for me the only source of real happiness and freedom, much as a child will put a backing of thick strong paper on a backgammon board that long use has severed at the fold. It meant, in a sense, a return to the poem without pain, a return to my private Golden Age.

Was I ignorant, then, when I was seventeen? I think not. I knew everything. A quarter-century's experience of life since then has added nothing to what I knew. The one difference is that at seventeen I had no "realism."

How wonderful it would be, I felt, if I could only go back to that omniscience in which I bathed as agreeably as in cold water in summer! Examining myself in detail as I was at that age, I found that the parts of me that my words had without doubt "ended" were extremely few, and that the areas polluted by the radiation of omniscience were very restricted. The reason was that, though I wanted to use words as a memorial, as my bequest to posterity, I had got the method wrong: I was cutting down on—even rejecting—omniscience, and entrusting to words the whole of my rebellion against the age. I was preoccupied with the task of making words reflect my body, even though I had none, and of sending them winging off towards the future, or towards death, bearing my longings like a carrier pigeon bearing a message in the silver tube attached to its small red leg. Even though one might be justified in describing this process as one designed not to let words come to an end, there was, nevertheless, a kind of intoxication in it.

Earlier, I defined the essential function of words as a

kind of magic in which the long void spent waiting for the absolute is progressively consumed by writing, much as embroidery slowly covers the pure white of a long sash. At the same time, I pointed out that the spirit—which, chopped into lengths by words, has its natural sense of the continuity of life constantly disrupted—is unable to distinguish a true end, and thus never knows an end at all.

If that is so, what function do words have for the spirit when it finally does become aware of the end?

An admirable example in miniature of what happens in such a case is to be found in a collection of letters, written by young men of the suicide squad before setting off on their last mission, that is preserved today at the former naval base of Etajima.

Visiting the museum one late summer's day, I was struck by the remarkable contrast between the majority of letters, which were written in an impressive, orderly style, and the occasional letter rapidly dashed off in pencil. As I stood before the glass cases reading the last testaments of these young heroes, I felt suddenly that I had resolved a question that had long worried me: at such times, did men use words to tell the truth, or did they try to make of them some memorial?

One letter that still remains very vivid in my mind was written in pencil on a piece of rice-paper in a youthful, almost careless scribble. If my memory is not mistaken, it was to the following effect, and broke off abruptly in just this fashion:

"At the moment I am full of life, my whole body overflowing with youth and strength. It seems impossible that I shall be dead in three hours' time. And yet. . . ."

When someone seeks to tell the truth, words always falter in this way. I can almost see him now, fumbling for words: not from shyness, nor from fear, for the naked truth inevitably produces this verbal stumbling; but, rather, as a sign of a certain rough quality about truth itself. The young man in question had no long-drawn-out void left in which to await the absolute, nor did he have time to wind things up with words in a leisurely way. As he hurtled towards death, his final everyday phrases seized on a moment when the feeling for life, like chloroform in the strange headiness it produces, had temporarily benumbed his spirit's awareness of the end, and, like a well-loved dog leaping up at its master, came rushing out upon him, only to be dashed rudely aside.

The neater letters, on the other hand, with their pithy phrases about duty to one's fatherland, destroying the enemy, eternal right, and the identity of life and death, obviously selected what were considered to be the most impressive, the most noble from among a large number of ready-made concepts, and clearly revealed a determination, by eliminating anything in the way of personal psychology, to identify the self with the splendid words chosen.

The slogan-like phrases thus written were, of course, in every sense "words." But, ready-made though they might have been, they were special words, set at a height loftier than any commonplace action could ever attain.

Once there were such words, though they are lost to us nowadays. They were not simply beautiful phrases, but a constant summons to superhuman behavior, words that demanded that the individual stake his very life on the attempt to climb to their own lofty heights. Words such as these, in which something first uttered as a conscious resolve gradually comes to demand an inescapable identification, lacked from the outset any bridge that might link them with ordinary, everyday preoccupations. More than any other words, and despite the ambiguity of their sense and content, they were filled with a glory not of this world; their very impersonality and monumentality demanded the strict elimination of individuality and spurned the construction of monuments based on personal action. If the concept of the hero is a physical one, then, just as Alexander the Great acquired heroic stature by modeling himself on Achilles, the conditions necessary for becoming a hero must be both a ban on originality and a true faithfulness to a classical model; unlike the words of a genius, the words of a hero must be selected as the most impressive and noble from among ready-made concepts. And at the same time they, more than any other words, constitute a splendid language of the flesh.

In this way, then, I discovered in that museum the two brave types of words used when the spirit has perceived its end.

Compared with these two, the works of my boyhood failed to get to grips with the certainty of death; with ample time to be poisoned by timidity, they were subject in equal measure to the assaults of art. I used words in a totally different way from those beautiful last testaments of the suicide corps. Nevertheless, it seems certain that my spirit, for all the freedom—license, even—it permitted to words, and for all the prodigality it permitted the youthful author in his use of them, was still, somewhere, aware of the "end." If one rereads those works now, the signs are plain for all to see.

Nowadays, I find myself speculating: the kind of life in which words appear first, followed by the body already corroded by words, was surely not confined to myself alone? I was surely, somewhere, guilty of a contradiction in rejecting my own uniqueness while affirming the uniqueness of my life as such; the unconscious education of my body should have made the contradiction quite plain to me. At that period, then, the "end" that the body foresaw and the spirit perceived must have been present in the suicide corps and myself in equal measure. I ought to have been able (even without the body!) to take up a stand at some point that left no doubt as to that identity, and among the young men who died—even, indeed, among the suicide corps—there were, beyond doubt, some who were eaten away by the white ants in the same way as myself. Those who died, however, were fortunately secure within a fixed identity, an identity established beyond all doubt—the tragic identity.

My omniscience at seventeen could hardly have been unaware of this. However, what I had begun was the attempt to remove myself as far as possible from omniscience. Determined not to use even one of the materials of which the age was built, I mistook obstinate persistence in my own views for purity; what was worse, I mistook my method too, and sought to leave behind a personal monument. How, though, could something personal ever become a monument? The basic reason for this illusion is only too clear to me today; at that time I held in contempt a life that could be ended by words.

Thus contempt and fear were synonymous in the eyes of the boy that I was then. In all probability, I was afraid of bringing it to an end with words, and yet, imagining that imperishability for words lay in escaping as far as possible from reality, I felt an intoxication in this fruitless action. One might say that there was happiness—hope, even—in the action. And when the war ended and the spirit promptly ceased to be aware of the coming "end," the intoxication also ceased on the spot.

What, then, could be the real meaning of my attempt at this late stage to return to the same point? Was it freedom I was seeking? Or the impossible? Or did the two things, possibly, come to the same thing?

What I was after, obviously, was a revival of the intoxication, and this time, in addition to the intoxication, I was conceited enough to believe that my technique in dealing with words was sufficiently practiced for me to choose impersonal words, thereby enhancing their function as a memorial and putting an end to life of my own free will. This—it would be no exaggeration to say—was the only revenge I could take on the spirit for stubbornly refusing to perceive the "end." I was loath to take the same course as others who, when the body is turning its steps towards its future decay, refuse to follow it but silently tag along after the far blinder and more stubborn spirit until they are completely deceived by it.

Somehow or other, I must make my spirit conscious once more of the "end." Everything started from there; only there, it was clear, could I find a basis for true freedom. I must soak myself once more in the cold water of my boyhood omniscience, fresh as a cold bath in summer, the omniscience that the misapplication of words had made me deliberately avoid; but this time I must give expression to everything, including the water itself.

That such a return was impossible was obvious without my being told. Yet the impossibility stimulated my mind in its boredom, and the mind, which could no longer be aroused to action save by the impossible, was beginning to have dreams of freedom.

I had already seen, in the paradox enacted by the body, the ultimate form of the freedom that comes through literature, the freedom that comes through words. Be that as it may, that which had eluded me was not death. It was tragedy that I had once let slip.

More accurately, what had eluded me was the tragedy

of the group, or tragedy as a member of the group. If I had achieved identity with the group, participation in tragedy would have been far easier, but from the outset words had worked to drive me farther and farther from the group. Moreover, feeling as I did that I lacked the physical ability to blend with the group, and that I was therefore constantly rejected by it, I desired somehow to justify myself. It was this desire that led me to polish words so assiduously, with the natural result that the kind of words I dealt in constantly rejected the significance of the group. Or should I say that the rain of words that fell so steadily within me during the period when my existence was barely adumbrated, like a rain that begins falling before the break of dawn, was, in itself, a forecast of my inability to adapt to the group? The first thing I did in life was to build up a self amidst that rain.

The intuition of my infancy—the intuitive sense that the group represented the principle of the flesh—was correct. To this day, I have never once felt the need to amend it. But it was only in later years, when I first came to know what I have called the dawn of the flesh— that rosy vertigo that descends on one after grueling use of the body and intense fatigue—that I began to perceive the significance of the group.

The group was concerned with all those things that could never emerge from words—sweat, and tears, and cries of joy or pain. If one probed deeper still, it was concerned with the blood that words could never cause to flow. The reason perhaps why the testaments of the doomed are oddly remote from individual expression, impressing one rather with their stereotyped quality, is that they are the words of the flesh.

At the moment when I first realized that the use of strength and the ensuing fatigue, the sweat and the blood, could reveal to my eyes that sacred, ever-swaying blue sky that the shrine bearers gazed on together, and could confer the glorious sense of being the same as others, I already had a foresight, perhaps, of that as yet distant day when I should step beyond the realm of individuality into which I had been driven by words and awaken to the meaning of the group.

There is, of course, such a thing as the language of the group, but it is in no sense a self-sufficient language. A speech, a slogan, and the words of a play all depend on the physical presence of the public speaker, the campaigner, the actor. Whether it is written down on paper or shouted aloud, the language of the group resolves itself ultimately into physical expression. It is not a language for transmitting private messages from the solitude of one closed room to the solitude of another distant, closed room. The group is a concept of uncommunicable shared suffering, a concept that ultimately rejects the agency of words.

For shared suffering, more than anything else, is the ultimate opponent of verbal expression. Not even the mightiest *Weltschmerz* in the heart of the solitary writer, billowing upwards to the starry heavens like some great circus tent, can create a community of shared suffering. For though verbal expression may convey pleasure or grief, it cannot convey shared pain; though pleasure may be readily fired by ideas, only bodies, placed under the same circumstances, can experience a common suffering.

Only through the group, I realized—through sharing the suffering of the group—could the body reach that height of existence that the individual alone could never attain. And for the body to reach that level at which the divine might be glimpsed, a dissolution of the individuality was necessary. The tragic quality of the group was also necessary—the quality that constantly raised the group out of the abandon and torpor into which it was prone to lapse, leading it on to ever-mounting shared suffering and so to death, which was the ultimate suffering. The group must be open to death—which meant, of course, that it must be a community of warriors. . . .

In the dim light of early morning I was running, one of a group. A cotton towel with the symbol of a red sun on it was tied about my forehead, and I was stripped to the waist in the freezing air. Through the common suffering, the shared cries of encouragement, the shared pace, and the chorus of voices, I felt the slow emergence, like the sweat that gradually beaded my skin, of that "tragic" quality that is the affirmation of identity. It was a flame of the flesh, flickering up faintly beneath the biting breeze—a flame, one might almost say, of nobility. The sense of surrendering one's body to a cause gave new life to the muscles. We were united in seeking death and glory; it was not merely my personal quest.

The pounding of the heart communicated itself to the group; we shared the same swift pulse. Self-awareness by now was as remote as the distant rumor of the town. I belonged to them, they belonged to me; the two formed an unmistakable "us." To belong—what more intense form of existence could there be? Our small circle of oneness was a means to a vision of that vast, dimly gleaming circle of oneness. And—all the while foreseeing that this imitation of tragedy was, in the same way as my own narrow happiness, condemned to vanish with the wind, to resolve itself into nothing more than muscles that simply existed—I had a vision where something that, if I were alone, would have resolved back into muscles and words, was held fast by the power of the group and led me away to a far land, whence there would be no return. It was, perhaps, the beginning of my placing reliance on others, a reliance that was mutual; and each of us, by committing himself to this immeasurable power, belonged to the whole.

In this way, the group for me had come to represent a bridge, a bridge that, once crossed, left no means of return.

EPILOGUE—F104

Epilogue—F104

Before my eyes, there slowly emerged a giant snake coiled about the earth; a snake that by constantly swallowing its own tail vanquished all polarities; the ultimate, huge snake that mocks all opposites.

Opposites carried to extremes come to resemble each other; and things that are farthest removed from each other, by increasing the distance between them, come closer together. This is the secret that the circle of the snake expounded. The flesh and the spirit, the sensual and the intellectual, the outside and the inside, will remove themselves a pace from the earth, and high up, higher even than where the snake-ring of white clouds encircling the earth is joined, they too will be joined.

I am one who has always been interested only in the edges of the body and the spirit, the outlying regions of the body and the outlying regions of the spirit. The depths hold no interest for me; I leave them to others, for they are shallow, commonplace.

What is there, then, at the outermost edge? Nothing, perhaps, save a few ribbons, dangling down into the void.

On earth, man is weighed down by gravity, his body encased in heavy muscles; he sweats; he runs; he strikes; even, with difficulty, he leaps. At times, nevertheless, I have unmistakably seen, amidst the darkness of fatigue, the first tinges of color that herald what I have called the dawn of the flesh.

On earth, man wears himself out in intellectual adventures, as though seeking to take wing and fly to infinity. Motionless before his desk, he edges his way closer, ever closer, to the borders of the spirit, in constant mortal danger of plunging into the void. At such times—though very rarely—the spirit, too, has its glimpses of the dawn light.

But body and spirit had never blended. They had never come to resemble each other. Never had I discovered in physical action anything resembling the chilling, terrifying satisfaction afforded by intellectual adventure. Nor had I ever experienced in intellectual adventure the selfless heat, the hot darkness of physical action.

Somewhere, the two must be connected. Where, though?

Somewhere, there must be a realm between, a realm akin to that ultimate realm where motion becomes rest and rest motion.

Suppose I flay about me with my arms. As I do so, I lose a certain amount of intellectual blood. Suppose I allow myself, however briefly, to think before I strike. At that moment, my blow is doomed to failure.

Somewhere, I told myself, there must be a higher principle that manages to bring the two together and reconcile them.

That principle, it occurred to me, was death.

And yet, my idea of death was too mystical; I was forgetting the plain, physical aspect of death.

The earth is surrounded by death. The upper regions, where there is no air, are crowded with death pure and unalloyed; it gazes down on humanity going about its business far below and bound by its physical conditions on earth, yet very seldom does it bring bodily death to man, since those same physical conditions prevent him from climbing this far. For man to encounter the universe as he is, with uncovered countenance, is death. In order to encounter the universe and still live, he must wear a mask—an oxygen mask.

If one took the body to those same rarified heights with which the spirit and intellect are already so familiar, the only thing waiting for it there might well be death. When the spirit and intellect ascend to such heights alone, death does not reveal itself clearly. The spirit, therefore, is always obliged, reluctantly and with a feeling of dissatisfaction, to return to its fleshly dwelling on earth. When it ascends alone, the unifying principle refuses to show itself. Unless body and spirit come together, the principle will have nothing to do with them.

At that stage, I had not encountered that giant snake.

Yet how familiar my intellectual adventures had made me with the loftiest regions of the sky! My spirit flew higher than any bird, unafraid of a lack of oxygen. Possibly, even, it had no need in the first place of anything so rich as oxygen. How I laughed at them, those grasshoppers who could jump no higher than their bodies would take them! The mere sight of them, far below me in the grass, would make me hold my sides and shake with mirth.

Yet I had something to learn, even from the grasshoppers. I began to regret that I had never taken my body with me into the upper regions, but had always left it behind on earth, in its ponderous casing of muscle.

One day, I dragged my body with me into a pressure chamber. Fifteen minutes of denitrification—the breathing in, that is, of pure oxygen. My body was overwhelmingly astonished to find itself placed in the same pressure chamber that my spirit entered every night, to find itself bound immobile to a chair, forced to submit to operations it had never imagined possible. Never had it dreamed that its role would be reduced simply to sitting, without moving hand or foot.

For the spirit, this was routine training in withstanding high altitudes, and presented no difficulties at all, but for the body the experience was unprecedented. At each breath, the oxygen mask clung to the nostrils, then detached itself again. "Look here, body," said the spirit. "Today you're going with me, without budging an inch, to the highest limits of the spirit."

"You're wrong," countered the body contemptuously. "So long as I go with you, then however high they may be, they're the limits of the body too. You only say that, you with your bookish knowledge, because you have never taken the body with you before."

But all such talk aside, we set off together, without moving from the spot.

Already the air was being sucked out through the small hole in the ceiling. An invisible lowering of the pressure was slowly beginning.

The motionless cabin was ascending towards the heavens. Ten thousand feet, twenty thousand feet. Though to the eye nothing was happening inside the cabin, that same cabin, at a frightening pace, was shaking off its earthly chains. As the oxygen thinned out within the cabin, so everything that was familiar and ordinary began to recede. At around the thirty thousand feet mark, some shadow seemed to be approaching, and my breathing became the gasping of a dying fish frantically opening and shutting its mouth on the surface of the water. Yet still my nails showed no sign of the purple of cyanosis.

Could the oxygen mask be working properly? Glancing at the "flow" window of the regulator, I could see the white indicator moving slowly in a broad sweep at each large, deep breath I took. The oxygen supply was coming through. But suffocation was taking place as the gases dissolved in the body were turning to bubbles.

So precise had been the resemblance between the present physical adventure and intellectual adventure, that so far I had not been alarmed. I had never supposed that anything definite could happen to my motionless body.

Forty thousand feet. The sense of suffocation increased still further. Hand in amicable hand with my body, my spirit was searching frantically for any air that might be left. Any air it found—even the smallest amount—it would have devoured greedily.

My spirit had known panic before now. It had known apprehension. But it had never known this lack of an essential element that the body normally supplied to it without being asked. If I held my breath and tried to think, my brain was immediately occupied—frantically occupied with the creation of the physical conditions for thought. And in the end it breathed again, though in the manner of one committing a necessary error.

Forty-one thousand feet, forty-two thousand feet, forty-three. . . . I could feel death stuck fast to my lips. Soft, warm, octopus-like death, a vision of dark death, like some soft-bodied animal, such as my spirit had never even dreamed of. My brain had not forgotten that training would never kill me, yet this inorganic sport gave me a glimpse of the type of death that crowded about the earth outside. . . .

And then, a sudden free fall. The experience of hypoxia produced by removing one's oxygen mask during horizontal flight at twenty-five thousand feet. And the experience of a sudden drop in pressure, when, with a brief roaring sound, the interior of the cabin was suddenly enveloped in a white mist. . . . Finally, I passed my test, and was given the small pink card certifying that I had undergone physiological flight training. Soon, then, I should have the chance to find out in what way the edge of my spirit and the edge of my body would meet and fuse together in a single shoreline.

The fifth of December was gloriously fine.

At the base, I could see the silver, gleaming forms of the F104 supersonic fighter squadron lined up on the airfield. Maintenance men were attending to 016, in which I was to be taken aloft. It was the first time I had seen the F104 so peacefully at rest. Often, with longing eyes, I had watched it in flight. Acute-angled, swift as a god, the F104 was no sooner seen than it had ripped through the blue sky and vanished. I had long dreamed of the moment when that speck in the sky would enfold my own existence within it. What a mode of existence it was! What glorious self-indulgence! Could there be any more glittering insult to the stubbornly sedentary spirit? How splendidly it ripped the vast blue curtain, swift as a dagger-stroke! Who would not be that sharp knife of the heavens?

I donned the dun-colored flying suit and fastened on my parachute. I was taught how to release my survival kit, and had my oxygen mask tested. The heavy white helmet would be mine for a while. And silver spurs were fastened to the heels of my boots to prevent my legs from springing up and breaking.

It was past two o'clock on the airfield now, and sunlight was falling and scattering from between the clouds like water from a sprinkler truck. Clouds and light together were disposed according to the familiar convention observed in depicting the sky over battle-scenes in old paintings. From some heavenly coffer behind the clouds, solemn shafts of light pierced through and fanned out towards the earth. Why the heavens should have formed such a vast, awe-inspiring, old-fashioned composition, why the light should have been filled with such inner weightiness, bringing a touch of divinity to distant woods and hamlets, I do not know. They seemed to be saying a mass for the soon-to-be-pierced sky.

I got into the rear seat of a two-seater fighter, fastened the spurs on the heels of my boots, checked my oxygen mask, and was covered with the hemispherical windshield glass. My dialogue with the pilot was interrupted frequently by directions in English. Beneath my knees rested the yellow ring of the ejection equipment, its pin already out. Altimeters, speedometers, instruments innumerable. The control stick that the pilot was testing was duplicated in front of me, and the second stick vibrated furiously between my knees as he tested his.

Two twenty-eight. Engine started. At intervals through the metallic thundering, I could hear, on a cosmic scale, the pilot's breathing within his mask heaving like a typhoon. Two-thirty. Gently, 016 entered the runway and stopped for a test with throttles fully open. I was filled with happiness. The joy of setting off for a world that was completely controlled by such things was something utterly different from the departure of an airliner, which serves merely to transport bourgeois existence from one place to another. For me, it was a farewell to the everyday and the earthly.

How I had longed for this, how intensely I had looked forward to this moment! Behind me lay nothing but the familiar; before me lay the unknown—the present moment was the thinnest of razor blades between the two states. How impatiently had I awaited the fulfilment of this moment, how I had yearned for it to come under conditions as strict and unalloyed as possible! It was for this, surely, that I was alive. How could I fail to feel affection for those whose kindness had made this possible!

For many years I had forgotten the word "departure," forgotten it as a magician might try deliberately to forget a fatal spell.

The takeoff of the F104 would be decisive. The upper regions at 10,000 meters that the old Zero fighters reached in fifteen minutes would be reached in a mere two minutes. Plus-G would rest hard upon my body; soon my vitals would be pressed down by an iron hand, my blood flow as heavy as gold dust. The alchemy of my body would begin.

Erect-angled, the F104, a sharp silver phallus, pointed into the sky. Solitary, spermatozoon-like, I was installed within. Soon, I should know how the spermatozoon felt at the instant of ejaculation.

The furthermost, the outermost, the most peripheral sensations of the times in which we live are bound up with the G that is the inevitable concomitant of space flight. Almost certainly, the remotest extremities of everyday sensation in our age blend with G. We live in an age where the ultimate in what was once referred to as the psyche resolves itself into G. All love and hate that does not anticipate G somewhere in the distance is invalid.

G is the physical compelling force of the divine; and yet it is an intoxication that lies at the opposite extreme from intoxication, an intellectual limit that lies at the opposite extreme from the outer limit of the intellect.

The F104 took off. Its nose lifted, then lifted further. Almost before I realized it, we were piercing the nearest clouds.

Fifteen thousand feet, twenty thousand feet. The needles of the altimeter and speedometer spun like small, dancing, white mice. Mach 0.9, almost the speed of sound.

Finally, G came. But it came so gently that it was pleasant rather than painful. For a moment, my chest was empty, as though a cascade of water had descended with a great rush and left nothing behind it. My field of vision was monopolized by the sky, blue with a grayish tinge. I felt as though we were taking a great bite of the sky, chewing it and gulping it down. My mind stayed as fresh as ever. Everything was quiet, majestic, and the surface of the blue sky was flecked with the semen-white of clouds. Since I was not asleep, to say I awoke would be wrong. Rather, I experienced an "awakening" as though another layer had been torn rudely off my wakefulness, leaving my spirit pure, unsullied as yet by my contact. In the unsparing light of the windshield glass I clenched my teeth against naked joy. My lips, I am sure, were drawn back as though in pain.

I was one with the F104 that I had seen before in the sky; I had transformed my being into this thing that I had seen before my eyes. To men on earth, who until a moment ago had numbered me amongst them, I had become a receding existence; I dwelt at a point that was now no more than a fleeting memory for them.

Nothing could be more natural than to imagine that the notion of glory derived from the sun's rays that poured so mercilessly through the glass bubble of the cockpit, from this utterly naked light. Glory was surely a name given to just such a light—inorganic, super-human, naked, full of perilous cosmic rays.

Thirty thousand feet; thirty-five thousand feet.

A sea of clouds spread out far below, devoid of any conspicuous irregularities, like a garden of pure white moss. The F104 headed far out to sea to avoid sending shock waves to earth, racing south as it approached the speed of sound.

Two forty-three p.m. From thirty-five thousand feet and a subsonic speed of mach 0.9, we climbed with a slight vibration through the speed of sound, to mach 1.15, mach 1.2, and so to mach 1.3 at a height of forty-five thousand feet.

Nothing happened.

The silver fuselage floated in the naked light, the plane maintaining a splendid equilibrium. Once more it became a closed, motionless room. The plane was not moving at all. It had become, simply, an oddly-shaped metal cabin floating quite still in the upper atmosphere.

No wonder, then, that the pressurized chamber on earth could serve as an exact model of a spaceship. The motionless thing becomes a precise archetype of the most swiftly moving thing.

There was even no suffocating sensation. My mind was at ease, my thought processes lively. Both the closed room and the open room—two interiors so diametrically opposed—could serve equally, I found, as dwellings for the spirit of one and the same human being. If this stillness was the ultimate end of action—of movement—then the sky about me, the clouds far below, the sea gleaming between the clouds, even the setting sun, might well be events, things, within myself. At this distance from the earth, intellectual adventure and physical adventure could join hands without the slightest difficulty. This was the point that I had always been striving towards.

This silver tube floating in the sky was, as it were, my brain, and its immobility the mode of my spirit. The brain was no longer protected by unyielding bone, but had become permeable, like a sponge floating on water. The inner world and the outer world had invaded each other, had become completely interchangeable. This simple realm of cloud, sea, and setting sun was a majestic panorama, such as I had never seen before, of my own inner world. At the same time, every event that occurred within me had slipped the fetters of mind and emotion, becoming great letters freely inscribed across the heavens.

It was then that I saw the snake.

That huge—but the adjective is hopelessly inadequate —snake of white cloud encircling the globe, biting its own tail, going on and on for ever. . . .

Anything that comes into our minds even for the briefest of moments, exists. Even though it may not exist at this actual moment, it has existed somewhere in the past, or will exist at some time in the future. Here lies the resemblance between the pressure chamber and the space ship; the resemblance between my midnight study and the interior of the F104, forty-five thousand feet up in the sky. The flesh should glow with the pervading prescience of the spirit; the spirit should glow with the overflowing prescience of the body. And my consciousness, that shone serene like duralumin, watched over them all the while.

The black shoulders of Fuji loomed in silhouette slightly to the right of the plane's nose, gathering their clouds in slovenly fashion about them. To the left, the island of Oshima, the white smoke from its crater curdled above it like yoghurt, lay in a sea that gleamed in the setting sun.

Already we were below twenty-eight thousand feet.

If the giant snake-ring that resolves all polarities came into my brain, then it is natural to suppose that it was already in existence. The snake sought eternally to swallow its own tail. It was a ring vaster than death, more fragrant than that faint scent of mortality that I had caught in the compression chamber; beyond doubt, it was the principle of oneness that gazed down at us from the shining heavens.

The voice of the pilot fell on my ears.

"We are going to lower our altitude and make for Mount Fuji. We'll circle the crater, then do a few rolls and lazy eights. Then we'll make for home, passing over Lake Chuzenji on the way."

Red lilies, reflections from the surface of the sea dyed crimson by the sunset, glowed through rents in the sea of cloud directly below. The crimson cast a glow within the thick layer of vapor, staining it with color, dotting it all over with red flowers.

ICARUS

Do I, then, belong to the heavens?
Why, if not so, should the heavens
Fix me thus with their ceaseless blue stare,
Luring me on, and my mind, higher
Ever higher, up into the sky,
Drawing me ceaselessly up
To heights far, far above the human?
Why, when balance has been strictly studied
And flight calculated with the best of reason
Till no aberrant element should, by rights, remain—
Why, still, should the lust for ascension
Seem, in itself, so close to madness?
Nothing is that can satisfy me;
Earthly novelty is too soon dulled;
I am drawn higher and higher, more unstable,
Closer and closer to the sun's effulgence.
Why do they burn me, these rays of reason,
Why do these rays of reason destroy me?
Villages below and meandering streams
Grow tolerable as our distance grows.
Why do they plead, approve, lure me
With promise that I may love the human

If only it is seen, thus, from afar—
Although the goal could never have been love,
Nor, had it been, could I ever have
Belonged to the heavens?
I have not envied the bird its freedom
Nor have I longed for the ease of Nature,
Driven by naught save this strange yearning
For the higher, and the closer, to plunge myself
Into the deep sky's blue, so contrary
To all organic joys, so far
From pleasures of superiority
But higher, and higher,
Dazzled, perhaps, by the dizzy incandescence
Of waxen wings.

Or do I then
Belong, after all, to the earth?
Why, if not so, should the earth
Show such swiftness to encompass my fall?
Granting no space to think or feel,
Why did the soft, indolent earth thus
Greet me with the shock of steel plate?
Did the soft earth thus turn to steel
Only to show me my own softness?

That Nature might bring home to me
That to fall, not to fly, is in the order of things,
More natural by far than that imponderable passion?
Is the blue of the sky then a dream?
Was it devised by the earth, to which I belonged,
On account of the fleeting, white-hot intoxication
Achieved for a moment by waxen wings?
And did the heavens abet the plan to punish me?
To punish me for not believing in myself
Or for believing too much;
Too eager to know where lay my allegiance
Or vainly assuming that already I knew all;
For wanting to fly off
To the unknown
Or the known:
Both of them a single, blue speck of an idea?